TABLE OF CONTENTS

CHAPTER 3

REQUIREMENT DEVELOPMENT 51

CHAPTER 4

INNOVATION AND R&D 72

CHAPTER 5

SYSTEM SAFETY 88

CHAPTER 6

QUALITY MANAGEMENT 99

CHAPTER 7

CHAPTER 8

CHAPTER 9

CHAPTER 10

CHAPTER 11

Preface

As an engineer for more than thirty years, I often hear enterprises talk about brand design, packaging, and marketing in the media and seminars, but I have never heard them talk about management, technology, and other related issues. This makes me wonder: is it a reliable brand when it lacks the support of management and technology? No wonder the word "brand" is often associated with market-related concepts for most people instead of a comprehensive effort within a company that a brand should possess such as business strategy, management methods, innovation and R&D, and implementation process.

I have worked in the national defense industry, aerospace industry, rail industry, and electronics industry as well as participated in many international large scale projects, establishment of management system, evaluation of vendor qualification, verification and validation of systems. From these experiences, I gained an understanding of business practices in many industries and international branded companies and, as a result, have made my own observations on how to build a brand.

Here are my observations: a brand is a sincere promise a company makes to the market, and the company has to do everything to keep it; a brand is a comprehensive effort and process of business administration; a brand is a long-term accumulation of reputation, and there is no shortcut for it. It is impossible to get instant results from all three of them. They have to be accumulated step by step. However, I have noticed that many companies tend to focus on external branding efforts like packaging, advertising, marketing, and storytelling rather than internal efforts, making it impossible for them to build a solid brand.

In light of this, I published the book "Brand Internalization Management (品牌內化經營)" in January 2016. It was later collected by the National Library of China and Taiwan's National Central Library which gave me great encouragement to write this book.

Introduction

BRAND is the accumulation of values!

Business models in the engineering and manufacturing industries have long circled around three things: minimum cost, maximum instant profit, and the lowest acceptable quality level. This has ruled out other more important quality and merits such as humanity, values, morality, and foresight. As revenue continues to increase, these three are used as criteria that make a traditional company in the manufacturing industry less likely to turn into a branded company.

There is an economic theory called "Pre-decisional Distortion" which refers to the phenomenon that the attributes and values that support correct decision-making are not considered thoroughly in advance and, therefore, the decision maker cannot achieve the anticipated goals and expected outcomes. This may be the exact portrayal of how "out-of-focus" many companies are when building a brand.

"Don't just ask how to do it but ask why." said Mark Zuckerberg, the founder of Facebook, in his speech at Tsinghua University in Beijing in 2015. If you do not know why you fight, there is no way for you to win, regardless of how many resources you have. Moreover, the spirit and soul of business are the starting point for all behaviors, so it is impossible to turn a traditional company into a branded company if you only focus on tools and methods.

After clarifying your purpose for pursuing a brand, the last few things you should try to understand are:

What is a brand? What is the difference between traditional management and brand management? What is the basic connotation of a brand? What is the value of a brand? How to build a brand correctly and successfully?

A company that pursues a brand should create brand connotation within the organization rather than only highlights the brand in the market. To do so, one should keep two points in mind: the brand philosophy and values at the management level and the value chain of brand performance at the operational level. The focus of this book is to give explicit interpretation to "Brand Philosophy and Values" and then to elaborate on "Value Chain of Brand Performance" that should be established within the organization.

The efforts of marketing, such as corporate logo design, image building, channel development, and advertising and endorsement, have been fully introduced and discussed in academic circles and in the market. The survey and evaluation of brand equity (including market share) are also conducted by many market research organizations. As a result, they are *not* covered in this book.

Brand value is the spirit of the brand building while brand performance management is the process of pursuing a brand and the way to keep the brand from failing. These are two sides of the same coin that cannot live without each other.

BRAND VALUES:

The cornerstone of character building

The core of brand culture

The shield to resist winds and waves of temptation

The criterion of operations management

Value Chain of BRAND PERFORMANCE:

The comprehensive program for the brand

The innovative thinking in performance

The management that begins with the end in mind

The end-to-end process

Chapter 1

Brand Overview

A brand is a comprehensive commentary on a company given by the public. It uses customer's *loyalty* and *market share*, the so-called *brand identity*, as indicators to substantially reflect customers' opinions. Loyalty is established by the process from brand recognition to brand awareness, and then to brand identity. It is a soft indicator presented by market research data. On the other hand, market share, a hard indicator, is the percentage of total sales in the market. Brand equity is a combination of both soft and hard indicators reflected in the stock market and M&A market.

The main difference between management in the branded company and the traditional company is that the ultimate goal for business management is to create the maximum profit, while brand management focuses on creating brand equity, including brand attention, reputation, association, loyalty, and market share. The latter is a combination of both tangible and intangible assets.

Brand identity is based on *brand awareness*. In other words, consumers must first have a certain understanding of the corporate culture, products, and services before they can feel a sense of identity with the company. The combination of both *brand reputation* and *brand association* is *brand awareness* which is the rational evaluation and the emotional response from consumers.

Before going into brand awareness, one should first pass the stage of brand recognition, the leading edge of brand promotion, which is generally achieved through corporate logo design, packaging design, channel strategy, promotional campaigns, etc., with *brand attention* as its specific indicator.

Brand building first starts from brand recognition, then to brand awareness, and finally to brand identity. So if one wants to build a corporate brand, one should not only establish *brand recognition* through advertising and marketing activities but also create positive *brand awareness* for consumers by providing high-quality products and services to create consumer experiences. When both brand recognition and brand awareness reach a certain level in the market, *brand identity* is naturally there. When the effect of brand identity is magnified and spread out, the company can make a brand identity loop as long as it adheres to its business philosophy and content to make regular customers purchase more and introduce more new customers.

It is the market identity that determines whether a company is a well-known and trusted branded company. So if the company wants to maintain sustainable operations, it has to constantly make progress to keep gaining market identity.

Every effort made by a company to maintain a positive market identity is called brand management. With this in mind, we know

- A company that sticks to advertising and celebrity endorsement but has a dishonest business model is not called brand management.
- A company that tells touching stories, which, however, have nothing whatsoever to do with its corporate experience and culture is not called brand management.
- A company that is good at profit making but disregards health and family happiness of employees is not called brand management.

- A company that develops their markets globally but does not pay taxes honestly, nor gives back to society is not called brand management.

A real brand possesses charm and attraction exuding from the core concepts of the company, not just the shining packaging designed by means of business psychology, advertising, and marketing.

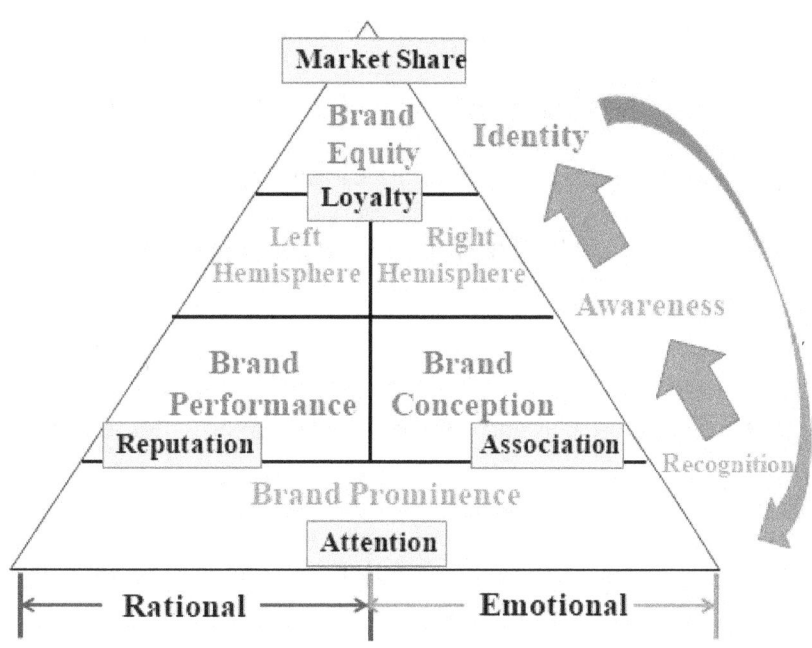

Brand Equity Model

In brand awareness, *brand performance* focuses on strengthening the reputation of the brand. A company can receive positive and rational responses from consumers through the establishment and implementation of nine core competencies. These nine competencies of brand performance are:

Requirement development, innovation and R&D, system safety, quality management, product and service suitability, logistics support, market service, system integration, and sustainability management. Detailed explanations of these competencies are given one by one in the following chapters.

What is a Brand?

"品牌(pronunciation: pin pai)" is the word for "brand" in Chinese. The first character "品(pin)" means taste, comment, and classification. So "品" is to let someone experience a thing, and then asks the person to make a comment or value the thing. "牌(pai)" is the image emanating from the characters of an individual or the value of an organization. Public opinion determines the level of value in a brand. Although it is possible for a brand to get popular for a short time through promotional strategy, all it gains is attention. We know time tries all things, so a real brand must go through the challenge of time which may even last up to a hundred years.

A brand is neither a temporary phenomenon, nor one single product or service, but the value that has been created and accumulated for a long period of time. The consumer who wants this value can satisfy their desire by purchasing the product and service. The starting point of the purchase is to buy the brand value rather than the product and service.

If a company's perception of a brand is nothing more than eye-catching corporate logos, fabulous packaging or gaining exposure, it is difficult for it to build a good brand. In addition to these external efforts, the brand building should not only be equipped with internal strengths that support the brand management but it should be also commensurate with the scope and the development process of brand reputation. Otherwise, customers are aware of the gap between corporate image and the products and services provided by the company, and, as a result, the brand cannot resonate with customers.

No matter which part of business management goes wrong, once the hypocrisy is revealed to the public, the brand reputation turns bad. For example, there was a hot pot chain claimed to only use high quality imported ingredients, and once the public knew they were lying—even it is not against the law—the impact of false advertising on the corporate image was nevertheless devastating. The company ended up scaling down its business quietly and going back to square one.

There was also a well-known listed restaurant chain, which claimed to be excellent in management and high bonuses surpassing many high-tech industries, held a sales promotion. However, the number of products provided was inconsistent with the expectations of the public and it even sparked off a major dispute. Moreover, the subsequent discussion touched on whether it is suitable for business owners to use the greedy nature of human beings to encourage more purchase and led to questioning the moral responsibility of companies. This case provides a very worthwhile topic for companies interested in brand building: to what extent do the values—other than business values—contained in the word "brand" should be presented to highlight and strengthen the brand and to avoid weakening the brand from conveying wrong values while marketing?

Brand Development Path

The growth path of the branded company is consistent and continuous. Fundamentally, "quality" is the first segment of this path. If a product does not even meet the basic quality requirements, the company must be falling apart, let alone building a brand.

Many companies with mediocre quality products can maintain their business, but this is as far as they could go, and there is no way for them to be an indispensable and irreplaceable company for consumers. Most of these profit-oriented companies believe in "business is business" and they have few corporate characters, such as having respect for humanity and contributing to society. What's worse is there are companies violate human rights, show no respect for basic human values, exploit their employees, confuse their customers with exaggerated statements, and even adulterate their products with poor quality materials—these behaviors are conducted without ethical standards and some of them are even illegal. Naturally, they are condemned and rejected by the public that makes it impossible for them to build a brand at all. Thus, "character" is the second segment of this path.

The third segment of the path is "taste" which strongly connected with values, cultural ethos, and how foresight and cultivated a business owner is. This goes far beyond the scope of business management. If the owner lacks appreciation and romance, then it makes it harder for them to run a sophisticated company. Taste is indeed an important element that resonates with real brand consumers because it is related to how cultured a person is. It reaches the level of self-esteem and self-respect that also includes the self-requirement for quality and character. This is why a person with a good taste naturally takes the brand seriously when running a business.

A company that adheres to quality is willing to delve into and invest in technology to maintain good quality. A company that adheres to character respects the law, moral values, and people, so it gives employees and customers fair and equal treatment. When cultivating taste, it shapes and enhances the cultural ethos from individuals to the entire company. Once these three elements are linked together, the company can then be sure that it is moving forward in the direction of branding.

11

The brand equity is resulted of these three steps. Quality represents the "nature" of products and services. Character represents the company's "nature" that shapes its behavior to fulfill its social responsibility. Taste represents the noble "nature" that fosters a culture in the market. With the presence of these three natures, the brand value is created.

Brand Attribute

Based on different attributes, the types of brands can be divided into three categories. The first one is popular brands which lose its appeal when products are out of fashion, such as the fashion industry. The second one is craft brands which provide a sense of trust and security to customers, such as the iPhone, Swiss watches, Mercedes-Benz, etc. The third one is cultural (boutique) brands which connect with taste that leads consumers into a hall of culture and history to indulge in a feast for the soul. This includes a wide range of business, such as art and literature, food culture, lifestyle, architecture, and even festivals.

Most of the well-known brands contain these three attributes that only proportionally differ in the business types and business models. It is impossible to quantify these attributes in a brand and cut them apart. A long-lasting craft brand, for example, can gradually bring in some elements from cultural brands or it can get closer to popular brands for higher profits by bringing fashion trends to its brand. Or, take popular brands as another example. Given its continuously changing nature that trends fade out and are replaced by new ones over a short period of time, if a branded company wants to create an associated element, instead of focusing on the market, it concentrates on the designer or the founder themselves, from whom the company creates its brand image leaving a strong and consecutive association for consumers.

12

The never-changing theme can, therefore, support the ever-changing products through this legend-building strategy—the legendary Coco Chanel herself is one of the classic examples.

Let's take a look at popular brands first. As the name implies, a popular brand has something to do with fashion trends, and fashion themes have instant explosiveness and attraction. But the needs of fashion consumers are changing rapidly and a fashion trend turns like a typhoon that no one can accurately predict. So for a popular brand, the key lies in whether a company can make a trend and stay ahead of the curve.

For a craft brand, no matter how technology develops, its skills and crafts should always stay ahead of the rest. But at times it also incorporates fashion elements in its products, such as a new application method of electronics or materials technology, and introduces them to the market through product placement. Whether it is in Knight Rider, James Bond, Batman, or Mission Impossible, those tools or weapons they used in these movies have all featured product placements.

A cultural brand is the collection of all elements in its original environment that deeply integrates with the historical background, living habits, value orientation, and even the ecological environment. A small change in it may cause the loss of the original taste and the fading of the brand. Since a cultural brand already has its brand effect, even when it comes to innovation, it must adhere to its core brand elements in the new one and keep its original classic version.

When developing a brand strategy, the company should fully understand the components of its own attributes and properly develop appropriate marketing strategy, product strategy, and service strategy.

Brand Value

The purpose of business management is to create profit, which, in short, is to increase orders, reduce costs, and create maximum profit—these are key business indicators. On the other hand, the purpose of brand management is to create brand equity which includes both tangible and intangible values, such as the identity and reputation created by the aforementioned character and taste. Therefore, brand management focuses not only on financial reports, production capacity and productivity, and costs but also on social responsibility, respect for human rights, and business ethics, etc.

With this comparison in mind, however, it does not mean that brand management is opposite to and in conflict with business management. The scope of brand management is more macroscopic that reaches a higher level and spans a longer period of time than the scope of business management. It strives for the sustainability of a company. Being a brand vendor means having more complete operational capabilities, so the long-term profit goes beyond business management. This concept will be explained later in this book.

The cause of the two Boeing 737 MAX 8 crashes in October 2018 and in February 2019 was that the company changed the engine and its position together with the corresponding control software so as to save fuel costs. After the first crash, Boeing refused to conduct a comprehensive review, which resulted in the second crash that eventually led to a global countermeasure against it. What safety and trust in exchange for is brand equity, not profit! Nevertheless, without safety and trust, you lose more money.

One can use money (cost) to make money (profit), but there is never an exchange of money for high market values! The noblest value comes from consumer's respect and nostalgia for the company rather than from the constant pursuit of profit. Connecting your business with eternal values as close as possible, then you can realize that the cornerstone of the brand is just this simple understanding.

When pursuing this value, you have to soldier on even when it shrinks the market and you suffer a decline in profits. It is because value, rather than profit, is in fact the reason that makes your brand business survive. The higher the profit margin is, the more competitors it attracts. In a competitive environment, you are either driven out of the market or overwhelmed by the small profit you make. Either way, it drags down your employees and their families altogether. For this reason, what a brand should grasp firmly is the value that wins people's heart, not the profits that shareholders pursue.

One may say: "so companies should *not* pursue profit?" No. The company should focus on making value rather than making profits, but value naturally brings in revenue which means profit comes itself. The harder you try to pursue profit, the farther it runs away. As Confucius said, "the gentleman devotes his efforts to the roots, for once the roots are established, the Way will grow therefrom," and this is also applicable to business.

The inconvenience of barter in ancient times led to the invention of money. However, when we are used to a world where value and money are linked together, over time, people project their value onto money, thinking that money represents all values in the world and eventually diminishing many other important values that are not measured by money. As a result, it fills up the world with realism and profit-oriented thinking that deprives of human values and even causes terrible tragedies.

The existence of brand management has partially reversed people's corresponding concepts of money and value. For products that made at the same cost, if the brand of the product A is better than that of the product B, then the price of the product A is naturally higher than that of the product B. In short, it is the value of the brand rather than the price of the product determines who the winner is. In recent years, the brand has been linked to human care. Since the profit of the brand is higher than that of the traditional company, needs to give back to society get stronger that unexpectedly connects with corporate philanthropy.

When the brand effect is large enough, many downstream or contract manufacturers struggle to be suppliers or manufacturers of the brand, thus the brand vendor has the right to determine the purchase price. Under reasonable quality requirements, they can purchase raw materials, semi-finished products, and finished products they need at the most reasonable price and sell their product at a high price that aligns with their brand value in the market.

From this point of view, the brand vendor holds the power to determine the reasonable cost and the ability to raise the market price. This is the implicit power endowed by the market.

Brand is the Heritage Passing down from Generation to Generation

Before a company is transformed into a branded company, it should first provide products and services that contain values deep and long-lasting enough so that the customer's memory never dies and can even be passed down from generation to generation. In this case, it is definitely not enough for products and services to just meet the correct specifications; they also need to give the consumer a heart touching experience that can remain deeply engraved in their minds.

People from the 1940s to the 1970s have the experience of using some long-lasting electronics and appliances. Challenges for these products were the needs for personal use, the requirements for simple and easy to operate, low prices, and durable quality. Even at a time when technology was not fully developed, these products could still meet the common needs of people. No wonder they could reach deep into people's hearts and be passed down from generation to generation.

After World War II, there were many new companies established with a good foundation laid by the first generation entrepreneurs while the second or the third generation could only maintain the success with relatively limited results. Why? The possible reasons are:

1. The spirit of dedication—the growing environment of these two generations is quite different which leads to totally different attitudes at work and leadership models.
2. Business administration—under the increased influence of capitalism, management models pop out like crazy.

3. Business change—trying to get rid of old burdens without knowing how to shape the new corporate culture.

4. Intensified global competition—even the management environment is different from the past, they still cannot get rid of the old business model to establish a new one.

5. The shortage of resources—it leads to the growing difficulties of business operations, especially the shortage of human resources from a substantial shortage to the embrace of news values. It is getting increasingly difficult for the company to protect and maintain its human assets, let alone enriching it.

Under the influence of modern business management, some successors have changed their concept of operations management, so materials were changed, service methods were changed, the decoration was changed, the taste was changed or the location of the company was changed. And they are scratching their heads about why their regular customers leave them forever.

So what is the problem? Checking for your brand elements is the key. If successors have different opinions, they may not maintain the critical and unique brand elements, which is, in fact, a devastating action that inadvertently undermines the business foundation laid down by the previous generation.

Since the market changes constantly, as time goes by, companies have to adapt to survive and progress under huge pressure; however, some basic elements never change. In order to develop new strategies on the basis of the existing ones, you must examine what the unchangeable brand elements of your company are and integrate these elements into the new strategic framework to establish innovative brand management methods.

Brand Performance is the Accumulation of Brand Value

When it comes to performance, it is important not to use profit as the most important performance indicator when building a brand because the pursuit of maximum profit leads to a series of decisions and judgments that value profit above promise, destroying the basis for building a brand.

When a company is guided by profit, cost minimization becomes its main focus. It produces a product that wanders around the lowest acceptable quality level in all aspects. Under such a situation, the occurrence of errors and flaws is unavoidable in the long run and customers are less likely to build full confidence in the company.

The other focus of the company is short-term business goals. In an attempt to avoid unknown risks in the future, it tries its best to make as many profits as possible, thinking it is safer to make a quick buck, and at the same time, this also helps it to attract more funds in the stock market. However, since the shorter the target period, the lower the stability of the business management strategy, this leads to the increasing chaos in operations management such as finance, human resources, production, and sales. Eventually, the company retracts or breaks the promise it made to customers.

The more determined the promise, the stronger the trust of consumers. The longer the trust lasts, the greater the brand effect exists. For the business owner who really wants to pursue brand management, it is important to establish performance indicators with a wider range and long-term targets.

The fundamental difference between the accumulation of brand performance and profit performance is as described above. When the brand performance is inconsistent, it loses customer trust. The profit performance, on the other hand, can be intermittent, which means the company can still fine-tune its strategy later even with a deficit in one quarter. However, once the trust is lost, it is hard to accurately predict how long it should take to regain customer trust. Simply put, brand performance is to accumulate customer loyalty, not profit!

A Boutique Is a Bridge between Value and People's Heart

Among the three attributes of the brand, cultural brand (boutique) has the noblest and most irreplaceable value which is believed to be the ultimate goal pursued by the other two types of brands. The boutique is the expression of shared ideas or culture, such as the value of cultural traditions, persistence in goodness, integrity, love, and the pursuit of excellence. When these invaluable elements become the connotation of boutique, the "absolute value" of money is therefore completely subverted.

The common connotations of boutique are the cultivation of humanity, the meticulousness in craftsmanship, the spirit of inheritance, the guarantee of quality, and the tacit understanding of taste. Moreover, it awakens customers' desire for enhancing their own identity by possessing boutiques. Since it takes a long time to develop a boutique brand which has years of carefully refined efforts in it, naturally, only those who know how to appreciate this boutique wholeheartedly can interact with it.

Since boutiques are equipped with the above values, they can shape a new social class. Possessing boutiques becomes a way of self-identification and a spiritual sense of belonging. Consumers in pursuit of popular brands are anxious to let everyone see them wearing or using these products to gain appreciation from others. But a true boutique owner integrates themselves with the value of the boutique and shares it with those who can appreciate its true value rather than show off to the public.

A culture boutique is not limited to goods but is broad enough to include—a variety of antiques; special traditional foods such as cheese, bacon, and exclusive production of fine wines; historic buildings or landmarks like the Louvre, Buckingham Palace, the Great Wall of China, and the National Palace Museum. It can be an activity as well, such as a ceremony, craftsmanship, performance or lifestyle. For example, the living culture of the American Amish people in 1700s, mahjong culture in Chengdu, snack culture in Taiwan, etc.

Although culture boutique is priceless, it does not necessarily mean the price is extremely high. The important thing is the value in it can last forever, and the longer it lasts, the more glorious it shows.

The first step for a modern company to transform into a culture boutique company is it should be classified as a legend in this era. This requires a very valuable innovation. The scale of this innovation is not necessarily large, but it must be unique enough to be the one and only innovation. The second step is to shape a corporate culture to maintain this *uniqueness* that cannot be easily changed over time. In other words, this uniqueness and the culture are interdependent and inseparable.

Every everlasting branded company does not survive independently without a supporting corporate culture, which withstands all challenges in all aspects. It must, for example, maintain a correct business philosophy, not to cross the ethical line, show consistent respect for humanity, offer a long-term warranty on products and services, contribute to society in a positive way, and reject the temptations of ill-gotten gains.

Craft brands and popular brands can also enter the hall of culture boutiques as long as they continuously gain consumer awareness in the market. Since culture is the appearance of life, once these two types of brands become an indispensable part of consumers' life, they can be classified as a cultural brand.

Boutique and Fashion

It is not necessary to make boutiques fashionable, but they must be passed down with their consistent core values. Boutique brands do not deliberately follow fashion trends because they have undergone and survived the challenges of market changes and time. Every element and process that makes a boutique has its own uniqueness, secretiveness, and persistence that is inherited from generation to generation. Some elements are not readily noticeable. Once an element is arbitrarily changed, the consumer can perceive the subtle change that changes the original brand identity, so the boutique loses its original appearance and therefore is no longer a boutique.

Moreover, a too fashionable boutique goes into the disadvantages of fashion, such as changing rapidly, being quickly ruled out, unbalanced production capacity, and abundant competitors. In case there is no precise control of these risks that leads to the destruction of the original brand values, it is like digging your own grave. Even if you want it to be a little more fashionable, it should be a timeless fashion, not a short-lived fashion trend. To be more specific, the boutique itself is an eternal fashion, not kitsch!

Conversely, in the event of innovation bottlenecks, popular brands sometimes borrow ideas or elements from boutiques to make a connection with customers as it tries to evoke good memories of regular customers' experience with the brand and at the same time creates fashion attractions for new customers. So it simultaneously triggers the desire to purchase for both regular and new customers.

Old school wineries never forget to mention that their newly introduced wine has been produced from old wine cellars. Even the application of the ever-changing electronic technology on the design of watches and clocks remembers to retain the traditional mechanical dial to trigger consumer nostalgia in traditional crafts. Under this train of thought, it is even easier to understand why there are more and more nostalgic restaurants on the street.

The reason why traditional classics can be the cornerstone of fashion is that everyone has their own childhood memories—could be their own experience or their parents' and grandparents' experience—immortally and deeply engraved in their minds. These memories gradually become reminiscence and nostalgia, and as people get older, the nostalgic mood gets stronger and stronger. At this time, they search for elements in traditional boutiques to find the consistency of habits or worship from the reminiscence and nostalgia. This is the power of boutiques that go through different generations.

~~ I don't do fashion, I AM fashion. —Coco Chanel ~~

Boutique is a High-valued Handicraft

In R&D design, the first piece is the one that gathers the most efforts with the best functionality, quality, safety, and reliability. It gathers the company's best resources and all attention. But this product is not for sale; instead, it is used as a prototype for mass production. Before entering mass production, there is usually a cost reduction analysis of the prototype that slightly reduces the quality of the parts, accelerates the process, reduces the weight of the product with lighter packaging, etc. By the time the specifications for mass production are determined, some of the best features of the first piece get eliminated as a result of compromising and the value of boutique disappears.

This distinguishes the difference between the first piece and the mass production piece. The first piece is the boutique while the latter one is the duplicated and degraded product. It takes resources, focus, and time, so it is beyond comparison with products that are either rashly launched in the market or sold at a ridiculously low price.

The production of boutiques is not all about the craftsmanship itself; other production elements also contribute great value to it. Most of the world-famous wineries produce wines that vary with different conditions such as climate, temperature, humidity, soil, and the duration of exposure to sunshine. These are elements that make their products so unique and, as time goes by, they can be transformed into boutiques. There is no way for mass-produced products to be comparable to it.

There are also some boutiques that rely on the process of ancient craftsmanship. They lose the value that makes them boutiques if they fail to adhere to these processes and their internal elements. Both the ancient Chinese swords and the Japanese samurai swords (katana) have their special refining process and ingredients, especially the skills of master swordsmiths. The inheritance of the boutique experience is only between the master and the disciple which is also one of the most important elements of the boutique.

There are also culture boutiques in high-tech products. Porsche only produces a limited production of hand-built cars every year. Once the advertisements are released, they are all sold out immediately and you have to wait for two or three years to get the actual car. Now you can see how powerful culture boutiques can be.

Boutique Only Exists for Those Who Appreciate It!

There was a well-known violinist played in a subway exit with a donation box in front of his feet in New York. Many people came and went without paying any attention to him, so after a few hours, there were few coins in the box. Finally, someone recognized him and paused to listen. It turned out that this man is a professional violinist, and the price for one ticket to his performance at the Carnegie Hall in New York is at least hundreds of dollars!

This experiment reflects a truth: he who does not understand the value of a boutique does not deserve to own it. Only the person who understands the value is willing to pay for it. Besides, the price is not only referring to money but also appreciation and satisfaction.

Of course, there are people who do not understand the value but are still willing to pay a high price, but this kind of "support" only stains the boutique. In the take-off stage of economic growth, there is a common phenomenon in all societies: a growing number of parvenus, who drive fancy cars, wear branded clothes, drink red wine, wear luxury watches, carry branded bags, and wear branded shoes, but make a racket in high-end venues. It is because they seek social prominence and try to quickly increase their social status, so they use money (tangible value) to buy the brand (intangible value) and decorate themselves. But unfortunately, since all that glitters is not gold, this reveals nothing but their rotten and empty inside. Seeing them wearing the boutique is like seeing a beautiful woman marrying an ugly husband that conveys a sense of awkwardness for everyone who sees it. With their boutiques consumed by such customers, the brand vendor cannot do anything but wear a bitter smile.

"When people have enough food and clothing, they know what shame and dignity are. When there are adequate supplies in stores, they know what manner and justice are," said Guan Zhong, the prime minister of Qi (one of the most powerful states) in the Spring and Autumn Period in ancient China. Or, in short, well fed, well bred. With sufficient materials, the idea of improving oneself naturally comes to people's mind, but there is something different between the inside and the outside. Solely improving the outside never increases the inside. On the contrary, once the inside has been improved, there is no need to use the brand to make up and decorate the outside.

A well-known barbecue restaurant once gave a less ideal demonstration: it launched a special offer that requires a specific coin in exchange for a buy-one-and-get-one-free coupon. Although it has indicated in advance that there was a limited quantity, it still enraged those who did not get to buy the coupon and triggered a protest. This example shows that it is not worthwhile to satisfy brand pursuing customers who possess no taste at all. The restaurant should be the innovator in products and services to create higher value and sell them to high-quality customers who can appreciate them and are willing to pay a higher price. Giving in to low-end customers only lowers your own identity and lets them drag you down to their level.

When a brand vendor puts in more efforts to meet higher-level customers' needs, they can actually enhance their own image.

On the other hand, as a brand vendor, if you tend to use sales promotion to lure customers, you leave a negative impression on the public and lose your taste and sense.

What is Brand Performance?

The first chapter of this book is coming to an end. It is time to talk about the second theme of this book: what is brand performance?

1. BRAND

A brand is an overall impression, comment, and positioning that people (an individual, a company or an organization) make or present to the surrounding environment. For example, character, product quality, service level, social contribution, and sustainability.

2. PERFORMANCE

With the goals set for the product, service or management process in advance, the degree to which the goals are achieved.

3. BRAND PERFORMANCE

Being developed under the brand strategy, performance indicators are targeted, coherent, completed, and capable of achieving the ultimate goal.

The communication between a brand and the market should pass the stages of recognition, awareness, and identity so that the contribution value of the company or the organization to the market can be fully accepted to receive positive evaluations continuously. Therefore, the achievement of brand performance should be the goal for branded companies or organizations.

As mentioned in previous sections, the total value of these three stages is the brand equity. There are nine core competencies for the establishment of this equity. Once a company takes them as performance indicators and connects them into a value chain loop that sets up a comprehensive process, it can gradually improve its brand performance and call itself a brand.

These nine core competencies are:

1. Requirement development: conduct needs analysis and development from complex conditions, such as cultural habits, ergonomics science, environmental conditions, future prospects, maintenance and support, and other services. Output: future outlook, environmental protection, energy conservation, and needs-driven innovation.

2. Innovation and R&D: conduct innovative research and design based on the collected or developed needs to provide new products and services with uniqueness, foresight, reliability, and a cost-effective life cycle. It gives the products and services most favorable competitive conditions. Output: new products and services ahead of market competitors that meet a variety of needs and conquer numerous challenges.

3. System safety: safety refers not only to product safety but also to comprehensive risks, prevention of risks in unsafe conditions, and the monitoring and processing of abnormal process. In addition to product safety certification, these are the key points that should be paid attention to.

Output: low accident rate, casualty rate, and compensation rate.

4. Suitability: the ability to adapt to environmental conditions, operational conditions, logistics and maintenance support in different weather conditions and regions before the expiration date of products and services. It aims to reach the highest level of customer satisfaction during this period of time.

   Output: minimum failure, fastest service, minimum cost for maintenance and repair within the life cycle, and customer satisfaction.

5. Quality management: quality is ubiquitous and is not just related to products. The quality of decision-making, organizational design, process, and human assets are equally important but frequently overlooked because the quality is mostly considered to be related only to acceptance criteria of a product.

   Output: qualified products.

6. Logistics support: the ability to fully support customers' needs during the full life cycle of products and services, together with the logistics support analysis and supply that can fully bring the suitability and services into effect.

   Output: right time, right quality, and right quantity.

7. Market service: provide customers with the fastest, the most economical, effective, and considerate service under support of comprehensive suitability and logistics support.

   Output: level of satisfaction in the market.

8. System integration: in addition to sustainability management, this refers to the ability and resources to seamlessly integrate the other seven competencies.

   Output: the ability to process and control information and to adjust conditions anywhere, anytime.

9. Sustainability management: the *soft power* a company uses to maintain its brand at a high level, including leadership, organizational learning ability, retaining

human assets, robust financial system, corporate culture, research and

formulation of the marketing strategy, business ethics and social responsibility,

and corporate values.

Output: the value of brand equity.

These nine competencies do not exist separately and independently; they are in

fact interrelated. Perfecting a single competency or some of them does not improve

the overall effect of the brand effectively. They must be fully understood, familiarized,

planned, managed, and tracked in the strategic management process to receive a

complete effect.

Formulation and Development of Brand Strategy

First, you have to determine what type of brands you want to be and then

develop your brand strategy:

- Know your enemy and know yourself. What is your product and service?
  Ask things about your core technologies, the types of products, the market
  price level of your products and services comparing to that of others, the
  range and attributes of customers, the frequency and depth of the customer
  dependency, etc. Last, use the same questions to evaluate your competitors.

- Clarify your market position. Decide whether to strengthen your product
  and consolidate the position, or to reorganize your army and make a big
  attack, or to take another course and create a new force.

- Once the determination is made, give a clear theme to your own products
  and services as the foundation of the brand. For example, quality, which
  means the quality of your product always maintains at the highest quality

level in the market; or it can be safety, technology, humanity, convenience, and of course, the best service.

- Figure out your customer base. Who will buy your products and services? Or, what types of customers are you willing to serve? At the same time, you should also decide what types of customers you do not want. They are customers who do not match your brand positioning and may otherwise have a negative impact on your brand identity that conveys misleading information to other customers. The intention of making a quick buck and raking it in regardless of the customer base is very ineffective and risky for brand building.

- Think about how to make all employees be united as one. Develop a training course for all staff that includes from the theme of the brand, brand policy, and corporate culture to how each department implements the brand spirit in day-to-day operations, and then make a lesson plan for long-term implementation. It should be the internal practice details of the company, not some random brand training packages from some random consulting firms. More importantly, it should be led by the business owner and managers at all levels to set a good example for employees.

Brand strategy in the decision-making level of a company should adhere to the concept of sustainability management, develop forward-looking requirements, and pay attention to service promises. With the brand strategy as the starting point, it can simultaneously develop three types of strategies that are on the same level as brand strategy together with the development of the nine performance indicators.

The roles of these three strategies and the nine performance indicators in business management are:

1. Brand strategy: establish brand values, brand positioning, and sustainability management.

2. Marketing strategy: business operators at the top management level should clarify the market position and the target customers to establish requirement development and the management systems for logistics support;

3. Product strategy: system managers (not just product managers) at the middle management level should focus on the development of innovation and R&D, system integration, quality management, product and service suitability, and system safety. Since needs derive from the market, not from the head of the R&D specialist, product strategy should follow the direction of marketing strategy.

4. Service strategy: customer service managers should first develop the strategy and model of products and services and ensure the implementation of logistics support. It is important for the service strategy to take both marketing strategy and product strategy into account at the same time to formulate a complete service system. It aims to bring good services to customers that make both the rational and sensible parts of the brand image integrate perfectly in customers' minds.

Through the brand strategy, the development of these three strategies, and the strategic positioning of the nine brand performance indicators, when all levels in the company work together and carry out their own functions—even the entry-level employees do their duties with diligence—the brand equity can then maximize its results.

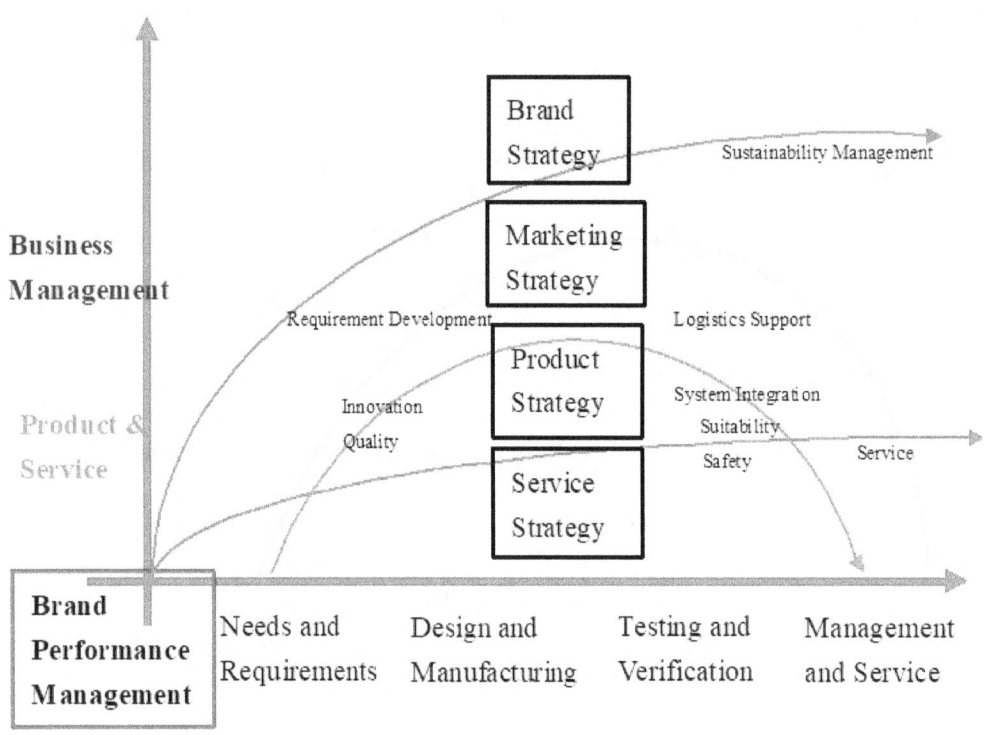

Chapter 2

Brand Value Philosophy

Based on the conclusions of *Chapter 1*, the basic idea of branding is to enhance and expand the original value to create a new one. Any effort that does not create brand value is a waste of time and resources.

What is value? In short, value is the degree to which one meets real needs. In order to meet needs, the seller must first create value in products and services and then puts a price on it; however, the price should be equivalent to the value, which means the seller should not price itself out of the market. It is profitable when the needs are met and the price is reasonable. The key lies in the correlation between the value the customer expects and the sales price of the product.

Long-term or repeated transactions occur when the consumer's expected value is greater than or equal to the cost they paid (i.e. the transaction price and the costs for subsequent use and maintenance). For this reason, when a company creates value for its products and services, it should also control the cost to make it less than the cost the customer expects.

But the question is: how does the company distribute the cost in the created value? Or, how does the company create the value that is more "valuable" than the original cost by adding extra efforts to the product? This is a great challenge for manufacturers who have long created value in the contract manufacturing industry. They are stuck in the middle of the value and supply chain where there are brand vendors that control the final selling price in downstream and suppliers that control the cost of raw materials in upstream. How much value can they create from contract manufacturing when they get sandwiched by these two? The answer is self-explanatory.

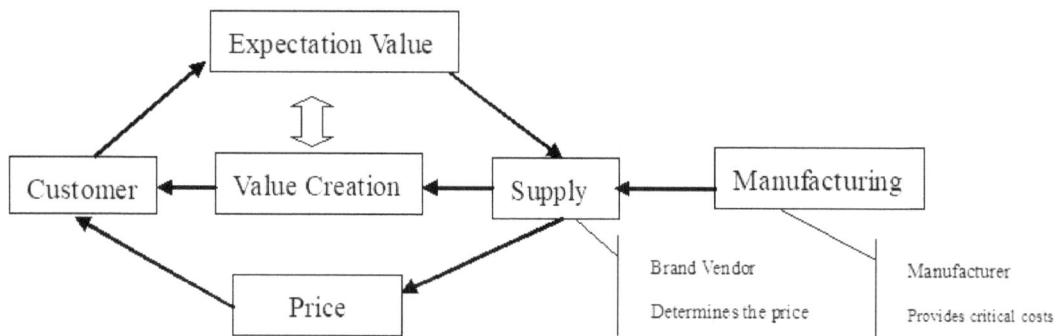

The Interrelationship Diagram between Price and Value

Value varies from person to person. The value of the same product differs from the purpose of use, identity, and time and space. For instance, it might be better for a convertible to be driven by young people than by the elderly, and it might be better for it to be driven on Sunset Boulevard in Los Angeles than in the desert. However, there are still general principles, such as good features, easy to operate, good quality, reasonable cost of ownership, comfortable, personalized, easy to maintain, feel respected and so on. In any case, value creation is to create an experience for the customer to feel touched and think it is worth remembering.

Sustainability Management

As mentioned in *Chapter 1*, brand performance is the accumulation of brand value. Trust and word of mouth are accumulated little by little over a long period of time, so get ready for sustainability management when branding, and then there has to be practical planning and implementation as well.

A branded company has overcome years of trials and numerous challenges in the market. These challenges include economic cycles, war and peace, technological innovation, the changes of habits and tastes, climate changes, the improvement of life goals, the importance of human rights, the increase of costs, the increasingly harshness of the law, and on top of that, the pressure from competitors. From these challenges, we can imagine how difficult it is to run a stable business for decades or even a hundred years.

Meanwhile, leaders at the decision-making level have also been replaced over such a long period of time. So what we should ask is which are the never-changing elements for a brand to carry on? Which are the ones that should keep up with the times?

The never-changing elements are elements that are closely related to humanity and basic social values that cannot be changed arbitrarily, including business philosophy, corporate values, vision and mission, corporate culture, and social ethics. If they are changed abruptly, it leads to the subversion of values, the disconnection from humanity, and doubts from the market that brings great risks to the company.

The business elements that should change with the times include technology, materials, design and manufacturing methods, application needs, taste, fashion, human rights, laws and regulations, energy and environmental protection, and corporate social responsibility.

To change or not to change, that is the challenge for branded companies. He who can control and soldier on this challenge is the winner. Secular values change with the times, and when not knowing the variables of the theme of the trend, a company with weaker resilience faces the choice of life and death. For example, the severe global climate change and global warming raise environmental awareness. Some of the most polluting industries founded in the early 20th century faced considerable political and environmental pressures by the end of the century. It is difficult for them to legally survive unless they spend more on pollution prevention and carbon emission reduction. Therefore, the company that wants to survive without increasing costs is basically walking on eggshells.

So do not blindly follow the crowd and promise easily to be a branded company. You get to know that this promise is not a matter of one or two years, but it takes at least thirty or fifty years long to fulfill it. Do not use media to beautify the brand because it gives nothing but a placebo. You might as well study the connotation and value of the brand, learn from other branded companies, slowly establish your brand management philosophy, and adjust your brand direction. Besides these, do not follow the rules of profit maximization. At the time when your company forms an internal brand culture, it has already become a branded company before you know it.

Promise Should be Clear; Service Should be in Place

For higher sales performance, the sales department often comes up with some advertising slogans or images that stimulate customers' senses and evoke their deepest desire. Under the influence of advertising, customers increase the value of the products and services they want to buy in their minds so high that they are willing to pay whatever they cost. It is understandable to use such an approach to improve instant performance, but the question is: how long can the substantive value keep in the customer's mind?

I have heard so many exaggerated advertisements. The real estate agent said it was situated three minutes from the highway interchange while it was actually thirty minutes. The medical sales representative said they could take care of all diseases while they took care of nothing. The clothing salesperson said it was made by international designers and it was the only piece in the world, but when you went to an international occasion, you found someone was wearing the same outfit as you. The dietary supplements manufacturer said it was Tianshan Snow Lotus while it was actually mushroom soften with liquid. The electronics salesperson guaranteed it could be used for ten years while it were actually broken down as soon as it was powered on. The waterproof paint manufacturer said it never leaked while it leaked when it rained. The cosmetics salesperson said nature was the best while it only contained trace amounts of natural ingredients. The cooking oil supplier said it was organic vegetable oil while it was actually animal feed oil. Are you sure your brand is real?

For the company that pursues profit, nothing matters as long as products can be sold out and there is no complaints and no returns received from customers. As for the company that pursues a brand, it considers how long does the customer feel satisfied with the product? Is it within the warranty period? Is it within the product life cycle? Or, they feel so moved that it last for a lifetime?

Selling products and services in an instant is not a very demanding challenge for it can be simply done through marketing and advertising. But there is a huge difference between this and to leave your customers with a heart touching moment that makes them come back for more and gladly recommend your products to anyone and everyone. If you want to achieve such an effect, the effort it takes is way different from short-term performance chasing.

Things that touch people's hearts can only start from the heart of people. We often use good listener, thoughtful, and considerate to describe good service, but the premise is that the service provider should agree with the value of the service and is glad to serve so they can pay attention to the customer. Nearly forty years ago when there were still car stewardesses on the tour bus, I took a tour bus on the Central Cross-Island Highway in Taiwan and there was this friendly and gentle car stewardess who helped each elderly passengers to get on and off the bus and she always made sure that everyone was seated before she blew a whistle to tell the driver it was safe to go. Having been to so many countries, this is the most impressive service I have ever experienced.

Instead of using service skills to make it look like a good service, you have to put yourself in people's shoes to let them feel grateful and make your service memorable. Indeed, the use of sales techniques or technology tools can be as impressive, but only considerate and thoughtful service makes people remember the touching moment for a lifetime.

Brand Value Only Exists in Customer Experience

The communication of brand value focuses on how to open and touch customers' hearts, not on how to properly use media tools. It is all about how the results of your efforts can go inside their hearts, remain in their memories, and bring positive effects—this is heart-to-heart communication. So what kinds of efforts can last forever in the hearts of customers?

First of all, transparency. When presenting correct efforts transparently in front of your customers, you can enter their hearts without saying a word. For example, a restaurant with an open kitchen. Or, direct marketing of fresh fruits and vegetables on which the buyer may seem to feel the morning dew. Nowadays, the Internet of Things (IoT) is increasingly popular which emphasizes the make-to-order (MTO) production, and it can have a great effect if it allows customers to track the manufacturing process and even get to watch it through live streaming.

With this straightforward communication style, it is very difficult not to get things done in the right way. If you want to establish a branded company, you may want to try this completely transparent communication strategy. The brand effect can simultaneously affect how the market sees the company from the internal management of the company. It is like killing two birds with one stone, so why not give it a try?

Another effort is proficiency, which means to take any situation that may occur into account in advance, think about what customers need, and prepare for these needs. In this way, customers can know exactly what to do next when using products and services, and it is even better if there are some necessary and proper reminders. For example, instead of providing a one-size-fits-all package, the real estate agent can prepare the related information and guidelines for customers to quickly find the best house matches their identities and purposes; industrial machinery manufacturers can plan an expansion program ready to accommodate upcoming technology for customers that helps them reduce reinvestment cost; the finance and insurance company can actively provide forward-looking risk management and hedging techniques for customers to reduce their losses. These are ways that can easily show how much you care about your customers.

The price is labeled for eyes to see while the value seeps into the heart without making a sound. When learning sensory marketing tactics and strategies, do not forget to learn how to contact and communicate with hearts. There is a design called perceptual design that aims to touch consumers' hearts so that they can feel the value of the product when they see it and generate a go-for-it feeling.

Bring Employees and the Company Together

One time I walked into the office building of a car manufacturer and saw there were all types of vehicles produced by the company parked in the parking lot. After asking the receptionist whether it was because the company sold their cars at a lower price to their employees. The answer was "no, it's just that our employees are all fans of our own products." I could not help but admire this company. Only when employees are proud of their own products can they make a joint and united effort for a better company.

The most uncontrollable thing for companies is that there are so many competitors in the modern society that constantly create and launch new products, so the choices for consumers are countless. Thus, when employees and their family members genuinely love their own products, they are the first group of supporters and the best endorsers for the brand.

There are companies host an annual "Bring Your Child to Work Day" for their employees, which not only brings the relationship between parents and children closer but also reminds employees to pay more attention to work because the achievement of work is also a parent's commitment to their children. At the same time, it allows supervisors to get in touch directly with these children to present the company's promise in front of them and increase cohesion between employees and the company. This wise approach is based on the idea of establishing closer labor-management relations other than that of paying attention to how much profit their employees can make.

There is NO Such Thing as Cheap and Cheerful

When it comes to real brand value, there is no room for negotiation because the value is accepted by customers who think it deserves what it costs. Those who do not agree with the value are not your customers, so there is no need to flatter them. Companies that are willing to use discounts to attract customers have already given in to financial goals and degraded themselves. After the first discount, inevitably, there is going to be the second one and more because savvy customers do not let go of any chance to lower the price. As a result, it is difficult to raise the price again.

Customers who bargain over every single purchase so hard that they do not stop until the sellers lose their shirt are the biggest destroyer of the market mechanism. This consumer power only forces suppliers to reduce their production costs lower and lower that not only results in poor production quality but also leads to deflation, lower labor costs, and a lower purchasing power that sets off a vicious cycle, causing a recession that affects the entire country.

This is why the common social responsibility of suppliers and consumers is to conduct transactions objectively and reasonably. This civilized trading behavior can encourage producers and service providers to continuously improve their quality and promote both their industry standards and their competitiveness. On the other hand, it also creates a prosperous economy for all people and boosts their income continuously and reasonably. By doing so, it plays a very important role in the development of the society, and this is just based on a simple change of mind that can make a great difference to individuals and the whole society.

Price is not a competitive advantage for a branded company—the insistence on quality is. For them, there is never a thing called cheap and cheerful because what they believe is "you get what you pay for." Based on this belief, they make the process of their production slow but strong, and they always take their time. If adding a new order makes them unable to catch up with the production schedule, they would rather lose the order because they know visionary customers will come back anyway, and these customers are, in fact, the ideal customers they are targeting.

Branded companies must get rid of the idea of cheap and cheerful, and at the same time, they have to make their products and services as good as they can and adhere to the value and price. By doing so, the brand creates a benign supply-demand cycle. This is what the universal saying goes, "there is no such thing as a free lunch"!

Time is a Test for Branding that Cannot be Hurried

One must first stand the test of time before one can build a brand. A company should work hard and go through ups and downs before getting popular. What kind of famous company or people can easily become a market darling? He who wants to be the one and only should first be able to see what others cannot see to create products and services that are unbeatable and unmatchable. This alone would make people struggle for a long time without any guarantee of success. There is no predecessor ahead on the road that leads you to be the one and only. It would be lonely and arduous for you to take on this road because, after setting a goal, you will be the only person who truly believes and supports you. This is especially true for all startups and there is no way for you to stop competitors from attacking and bashing you.

The advent of change is inevitable even for a long-standing company with a large market share. At this time, it is challenging enough when the successor and the previous generation share different ideas and concepts on how to manage the company, let alone the copying and attacking from competitors. The successor may change the old culture, or the successor may be swallowed up by it; either way, this is definitely a struggle for the company. On top of that, whether the old senior executives can adapt to the successor's leadership style—either submit themselves to the new leader or organize a secret rebellion—affects the company to some extent. Furthermore, it has to wait until the internal adjustment is accomplished before it regains its foothold in the market.

Almost all traditional branded companies gain a foothold in the local market first and then slowly expand their markets by word-of-mouth effect. Although this development process is exhausting, the management is relatively easy, and they can gain support from the family. After the advent of e-commerce, patterns of commercial competition have changed dramatically. The old marketing rules like the 4P (Product, Price, Place, and Promotion) has been greatly reduced and replaced by the 4E (Experience, Expense, E-Shop, and Exhibition). Marketing techniques have changed drastically as well, which is not only difficult for the previous generation to integrate but it is also not easy for the successor to be able to grasp its essence and use it effectively. They have to adopt the learning-by-doing approach and absorb new knowledge to explore and move forward.

Running a business is also like sailing against the wind; either you keep forging ahead or you keep falling behind. As globalization is getting faster, there are all kinds of challenges beyond anyone's imagination, and it is impossible to build a strong brand without standing the test of time!

The Name Must Match Reality

There was a fast-growing bakery claimed they only used healthy ingredients, but some customers broke the news saying they just used some ordinary ingredients. This is a typical case of keeping up with the Joneses which also reveals the fact that the manufacturer already had the concept of the brand, but they applied it wrong.

Why could not they just be honest? To put it bluntly, they deliberately misused brand knowledge to seek maximum profit. This manufacturer lacked another more important brand element—character. Do you remember the path of brand building in *Chapter 1*? They were still only halfway to the brand, yet they got stuck.

There was a big company that hired a world-renowned marketing guru to be the CEO who, however, regarded the channel as the terminal market and counted the goods sent to channels as part of their sales performance. This made the brand marketing strategy seem like a success at first, but it was until the annual settlement did it turn out that there were not so many purchases made as expected. On the contrary, because of overproduction, there was a large amount of bad debts accumulated that ended up being recorded as an inventory loss. This is how it looks like when reality does not match the name!

Do Not Violate Universal Values

What is universal value? The basic ones are: respect for the law, the principle of good faith, the right to life and health, protecting ecosystems, respect for human rights (including gender, age, work, social status, ability, disability, and sexuality), the principles of equality and non-discrimination, respect your competitors, etc.

Respecting universal values is only one of the most basic principles for branded companies, and it is also one of the foundations for the corporate character. Once you appear to have no respect for universal values, the trust of customers disappears immediately and it is unrecoverable no matter how great your business management is.

The situations of violating universal values are obvious at a glance. Let's look at some plausible and implicit cases: some companies make alluring offers with higher salaries to the employee of their competitors, and the situation is reversed at once. Those people who are previously poached definitely get kicked out once they are useless. Conversely, these companies are often betrayed by their own employees for the lack of integrity in their corporate culture.

Another example is there are social climbers who use the so-called "standing on the shoulders of giants" to ingratiate themselves with politicians. In some less serious cases, they seek protection from these political figures to protect their interests; in other more serious cases, with the collusion between business and government, they can make a killing. They often invest lots of money in politics to expand their business—let's just put the violation of the principle of fair competition aside—if the business causes damage to the lives and property of the people, together with the fact that the company is backed by a political party, it is going to be a huge disaster that may destroy the country and its people.

Specifications Should be Clear

The specification is neutral. It can be called as a perfect deal only when both buyer and seller come to an agreement on the specification they think is reasonable and accept it truthfully. If there is any defect in the contract such as ambiguity, deception, and opaque process, it leads to disputes between the two parties in the end.

There are two types of unfairness in contractual behavior. The contract in the seller's market must be biased towards the seller that usually leads to an asymmetric situation where the seller dominates the buyer. After tons of pages, many contracts of large or high-value products are written at the end of the contract as: all pictures shown are for reference only. Actual product may vary. Or: we do not take any responsibility for… and we are not liable for any damage caused …, etc.

There is also another kind of seller who controls everything. They may not necessarily deceive the buyer, but the seller has the final say whether it is on the price, quality, usage and maintenance approaches or even when the equipment renewal should be. In this case, the buyer can only swallow their pride and get ripped off unless they are capable of making products on their own. Now you can see how important industrial strength is!

The contract in the buyer's market is biased toward the buyer, which is the second type of unfairness, and since the buyer can dominate the seller, it gives the buyer a chance to make endless demands—asking for more, asking for gifts, waiting on their hand and foot, and even reserving the right to make unrestricted requirements in the future. There is a type of contract written like this: the content of this contract shall include, but not limited to: …! What do people who are familiar with business operations think when seeing this contract provision? There is no upper limit of the cost. What about the profit? Will the buyer add more budget?

The purpose of fair trade is not just about fairness itself; there is also the purpose of preventing deeper and more negative impacts. When the seller makes the buyer lose out, it leads to financial shocks which makes the buyer lose their life savings, end up in huge debt or lose their dependence of life and become a social burden. On the other hand, when the buyer makes the seller lose out, the seller falls into a nightmare that has no end, and they have no choice but to use inferior materials to produce products or to get served with a lawsuit for a long time, delaying the whole service forever.

Greed and Fraud

Advertising slogan that makes consumers' hearts pound with excitement is usually something that says it can bring you money all the time, like "bring a ten thousand-fold profit" or "make money while sleeping." The type of goods that misguide people on purpose and lure them with temptation is always nothing but financial derivatives, spiritual goods, and political promises.

There is a common character in these goods, that is, it is not easy to control and measure its process so that people have to use their imagination to support the value. Of course, the person who sells them must be very persuasive and eloquent with the ability to put flesh on the imaginary and empty content of the goods, making the buyer glad to give everything they have to get it. What makes things worse is that they take advantage of their consumers' information or their knowledge gaps to sell empty imaginations and make people even squander their nest egg.

Another form of fundraising is to satisfy the needs of the mind by providing a mysterious theory and various training methods to confuse people and create a supreme value and belief to attract great dedication or investment. What comes next is something related to the spiritual practice such as accessories and diets that are claimed to be gone through certain spiritual purification that makes their price outrageously high. Many people who believe in it are even well-educated people that perfectly shows how the mind is priceless but ignorant.

False advertisements and greed are two sides of the same coin. Any unreasonable high return always ends up bringing regret and vexation to the deceived one.

Give Customers a Product They Can Use for a Lifetime

Modern business administration pursues profit maximization, thus there are companies provide products that have been taken their durability into account to prevent the quality from failing within a specific period of time that has been precisely calculated. What's more incredible is that the technology for quality control can even make the failure show up in valuable parts, so that the cost of repair can be nearly as much as the price for a new one that makes the customer decide not to repair the old one. However, since there are too many choices in the market, coupled with the fact that for customers, new things are always more attractive than old ones, they often choose another manufacturer. So obviously, this trick does not seem to work as effectively as they expect.

I once bought a branded television for its five-year warranty. Time flew so fast and one day it was broken, so I sent it back to the manufacturer. After the inspection, the technician informed me that the warranty period has just expired, and the repair cost was near the price of a new TV. I had no choice but to buy a new one, but this time I switched to a different manufacturer. The feeling of being meticulously calculated and forced to buy is really unpleasant which, by the way, is not so much a clever strategy. But do not ask me how I can tell if this strategy is good or bad, all I can tell you is this brand has disappeared from the market for a long time.

One of my deepest childhood memories is the watches used in my father's generation, all Swiss Rolex, which were still very punctual even with a yellowed surface. As for fountain pens, most of them were Parker IM; the body of the pen was rough and mottled, but somehow, there was an infinite imagination and inexplicable admiration in it. At that time, parents gave a Parker IM fountain pen for their children at every important stage of development to record the user's life, so the pen was closely linked to the user and it was also served as a reminder for future generations to remember. They are products that deserve to be called a "Brand".

Chapter 3

Requirement Development

It is difficult to fully describe *needs*. Let me ask you: when you were using an 8-bit desktop computer thirty years ago, did it ever strike you that there would be a laptop or a tablet that you could carry around thirty years later? Or, when you were riding a Vespa scooter imagining you were Joe Bradley in *Roman Holiday* thirty years ago, did it ever occur to you that one day you would drive an electric vehicle that would not release carbon dioxide?

The truth is, you do not really know exactly what you need which is generated by multiple sources, including the random stimuli generated internally. How a company can accurately predict and define the needs, provide solutions to them, and find the direction of its business?

The sources of *needs* are numerous; they can be basically divided into basic survival needs, the needs to counter the natural and man-made threats, the needs for social and cultural activities, and psychological needs. Old companies with stable revenue lose the ability to develop new needs when they take customers' needs for granted. As for new companies, what they have to do is to find, concentrate, and attract these needs to improve their innovation capabilities to satisfy consumers' appetite.

Needs can be created, motivated, and guided. It depends on whether the proposed new needs are touched people's hearts and the newly launched products are more attractive than the previous ones. The next step is whether the company is able to always take the lead in demand innovation and make the quality and service of the production simultaneously maintain at the same level. It is no wonder people say it is difficult to stay in the lead since one has to stay motivated intensely and rigorously all the time.

The crucially important need is safety and survive. So in a dangerous situation, if there is something that is life-saving, everyone will definitely and immediately pay for it!

Sources and types of needs:

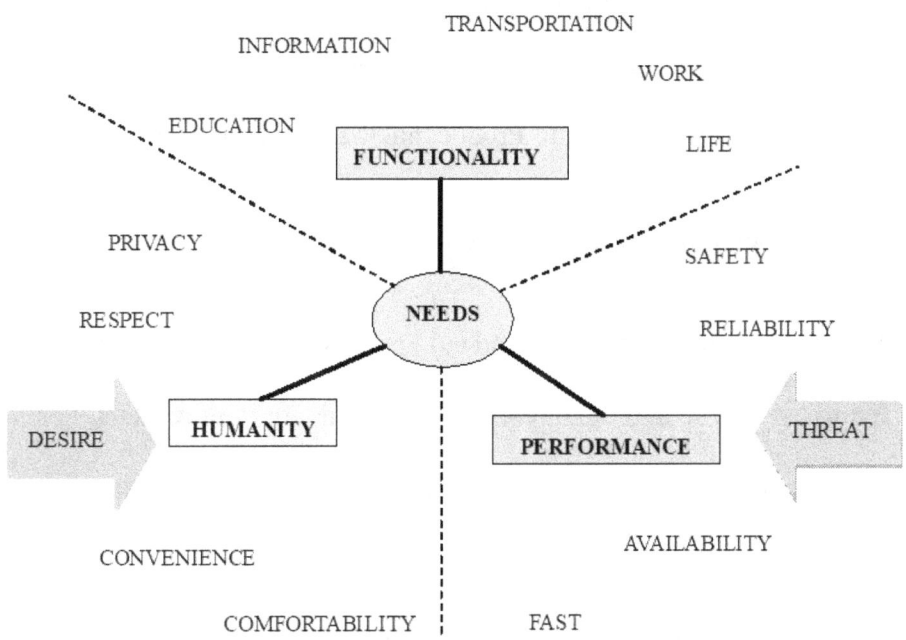

Needs must be converted into a product and service system, which is shown in the following flow diagram together with the subsequent instructions:

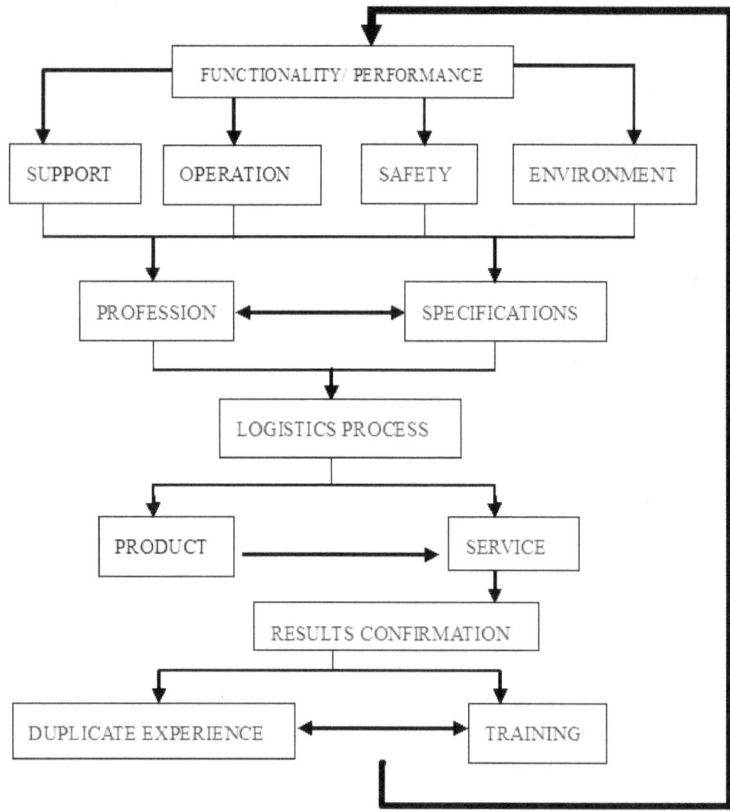

Converting Needs into Product and Service Processes

➢ Five key considerations for the product to meet the needs:

✓ Take the natural environment and culture of the local area into account to figure out how to avoid unfavorable conditions for your product. For example, you certainly know that it is impossible to sell ice machines to Alaska and heating machines to Africa! However, you may neglect the electrostatic effect caused by dry conditions that in turn causes electronic circuit failure and damages the device without even knowing it.

✓ Take the effects of changes in operating conditions into account, such as operating time, operating range, the upper and lower limit of content or quantity, etc. For example, an electromechanical equipment supplier supplies products to a backward country. According to the normal operation of the product, it should be performed basic maintenance after 1,000 hours of operation, intermediate maintenance after 10,000 hours of operation, and advanced maintenance after 50,000 hours of operation. However, the operator ignores all maintenance levels for more production, so it has an adverse effect on the life of the equipment. Moreover, the equipment supplier does not have a deep understanding of the user's operations strategy to take countermeasures, and consequently, it leads to customer dissatisfaction.

✓ Take the effects of changes in operational methods into account, such as speed, turnover interval and limits, and ergonomic adaptation to the operator and the user. For example, for higher performance, an amusement park adjusts the scheduled operation process to speed up recreational facilities in the hope of increasing the passenger turnover. But by doing so, it not only reduces the quality of the equipment but it also increases the risk of amusement park rides to tourists.

✓ Take support needs into account, such as the number and the life cycle of consumables, the quality and quantity of service staff, the maintenance methods and cycles, the supply support of equipment and materials and so on. The support service generated by the three needs mentioned above relates to the supply of raw materials, spare parts, and service staff. Designers can design according to the given standard specifications, but since the environmental and operational effects are not unchangeable, the support for products and services should take the range of these variables into account. In this manner, with the use of elastic design, the support can be optimized; furthermore, by strictly defining the upper and lower limit of the equipment, the operator can follow the schedule without causing any legal disputes.

- ✓ Safety assessment is the last and the most important one. Without safety, nothing else matters. If the product or the service is not safe, then all the business operations have no meaning. Normally, if a senior executive expresses certain subjective interest in product direction, the feasibility study made by the subordinates adopt a positive attitude to cater to the senior executive and make suggestions and draw whatever conclusions they preferred. However, their disregard for actual risks leaves the risk of causing injury to customers, customer claims, and the loss of reputation in the future.

➢ Conversion of *needs*:

- ✓ Profession: according to professional attributes of different *needs*, a professional team of experts from different fields has to examine the appropriate range of application and connotation of *needs*, and convert them into applicable and executable specifications.

- ✓ Specification: used as a basis for the designer and manufacturing process planning, specification is converted from *needs* through professional analysis or the selection of existing technical standards.

➢ R&D and manufacturing process:

This is the process of realizing *needs and specifications*. It is also known as the middle part of the industry value chain, which is the middle part (bottom) of the smiling curve. If you work in this manufacturing part, then you are working in the so-called contract manufacturing industry.

- ✓ R&D: use the analytical conclusion of all needs and the converted specifications mentioned above as the basis for R&D and the desired objectives and outcomes.

✓   Manufacturing: bring the research and development results into reality.

➢   Confirmation of results:

At this stage, it should fully confirm whether the needs mentioned above and the converted specifications are completely achieved in the design and manufacturing stage. There are five stages of confirmation:

✓   Analysis and evaluation

✓   Simulation and testing

✓   Design review

✓   Manufacturing inspection

✓   Correction and improvement

➢   Mass production and training:

✓   Mass production: the capacity control for the mass production process

✓   Training: operations and maintenance personnel training

The range of *needs* also involves how to get products and services into the hands of customers; the period from that time until products are discarded and then create new needs. This part includes product packaging, marketing channel, point of sale, and after-sales service which varies among different products and services. For more information, please see *Chapter 9*.

There are nearly seven billion of "me" in this world. Customers live in yours and hundreds of others' brands, so you have to continuously absorb and accumulate personalized experience before you can succeed. Branded companies should be more attentive to learn more about brand enthusiast behavior and interaction with customers.

The First Priority of Business—Understand the Needs of Customers

When you are excited to increase your brand exposure, think about the following questions first to see if you overlook anything: what does the customer think of your products after seeing them? Which one do you want to attract, the customer or yourself? Carry out more market evaluations, observe the reactions and responses of your customers, and slowly get rid of subjective opinions after repeating these processes. By doing so, you can completely put yourself in the customers' shoes to see what do your products and services look like from their perspective, and then truly understand what they want.

Your business does not exist if you do not even know who your customers are and what they really need! There is only one starting point for business—understand the needs of your customers!

It is difficult enough to observe changes in needs; it takes way more efforts and time to observe long-term changes in needs.

Regardless of whether there is a tool for collecting market information, what you should be concerned with is: whether all managers of the company keep every tiny clues of the customers' needs in their minds? How does marketing and business departments collect, organize, and analyze market information? How are these messages being interpreted and converted into business indicators? Have these business indicators been converted into performance indicators for every department? And finally, are these performance indicators assigned to each work process and output within the company? Only when you focus on the needs of customers all the time can you gain long-term loyalty from them.

Many years ago, I participated in a major project, which had not been made any progress for almost a year. After I took over for a while, the project was getting back on track. One day my supervisor told me: "you know, we have a meeting with our clients once in a month, and before you took over the project, it was the only day in a month we were busy with arguing with clients while there was nothing else for us to do in the rest of the month. But since you took over the project, we have been so busy every day, and we can only give us a break in that meeting day, and that is why there is no fighting anymore." This gave me rather mixed feelings and I really did not know how to respond.

You do not have to spend extra money on listening to your customers. All you have to do is to make sure whether their voices gathered from various departments form a data receiving network within the company to get every piece of data all the time. These direct or indirect messages are disclosed by customers spontaneously at different hierarchy levels in different places at different time. However, the voice of the customer is often weakened and even dies away due to the fact that the division of labor and the decentralization within the organization are inclined to block them. If you want the voice of the customer to be heard in the organization, just make up your mind to break the existing organizational "boxes," establish a spider-web-like mechanism for collecting and gathering data, and then carefully analyze it. After confirming that the need is true and can make a positive contribution to the increase of brand value, deal with it immediately.

Localization is the Starting Point

Have you ever had this experience before? After you saw a newly opened small restaurant, you went inside to give it a try. If it tasted good, you became a frequent customer. Meanwhile, the restaurant's business was getting better and its reputation slowly spread by word of mouth.

But gradually, the taste was not the same anymore and the store lost the elements that attracted you in the first place while the decoration was getting more and more glorious and the advertising was getting bigger and bigger. There were lots of visitors from other places came here to catch up with this trend. At this time, you never went back to this restaurant again but went back to the old vendors you were familiar with instead.

The Yong He Soy Milk shop, which is well-known in Taiwan and China, was established decades ago by several veterans who came to Taiwan with the National Government of the Republic of China. When they retired from the military, they did not get much military retirement pay due to the government's financial difficulties. Several veterans just set up a shed in an open space in Yong He, Taipei, to sell the most popular and common breakfast in their hometown. Its excellent taste has made the popularity soar and left a deep impression for many people in Taipei. Many years later, people grew up and left their hometown, but when they returned to Taiwan, they always went to this Yong He Soy Milk shop to have a piece of Clay Oven Roll and Fried Bread Stick and then drink a bowl of smooth soy milk as a cure for their homesickness. Decades later, it has become a well-known breakfast brand for Chinese people throughout the world.

There are so many other well-known foods or specialties from all over the world that are deeply rooted in the hearts of the people in the olden days. After they became famous, they either remain in the same place to innovate or expand outwards, but somehow, the original taste is gone, leaving it existing in the memories of the elderly who cannot show any evidence when they want to tell their descendants about those times. These old brands just disappeared like that.

Remember your original goals! Do not turn your business into a profit-oriented one after it gets prosperous. Do not lose your original sincerity and taste that brings you success and abandon your regular and loyal customers. Over time, when all the local customers leave you, you end up losing your identity in the market.

Always Pay Attention to the Changes of Needs

There are numerous sources of needs and the changing elements of needs are also intermixed with each other, including scientific and technological progress, new material research and development, improvement of technical skills, application changes, improvement of living standards, identification, the free flow of information, customization, environmental change, new concepts of health, and new lifestyle. These are elements that should be considered as much as possible when creating new needs.

The emergence of full touch screen mobile phones and tablets completely overturns the traditional push-button mechanism, allowing the operation mode to be easily used by consumers of all ages. What's more astonishing is that some newly developed products do not come with a screen, but directly project the contents on any surface or even display them in the air with stereoscopic 3D technology. The user can give operational commands by touching it. It can reduce many problems that come with interface elements, such as the manufacturing materials, the cost, and non-biodegradable waste management. This product is a very successful example of demand innovation that simultaneously achieves the goals of simplifying the user interface and protecting the environment.

With the advent of global aging in both developed and developing countries, various assistive devices, from traditional mobility aids to the electric mobility aids, are developing rapidly which greatly meets the needs of the elderly and reduces legal problems caused by hiring foreign caregivers.

Needs are hidden in various races, genders, and age groups that flow slowly like ocean currents. Whether to go with the flow or to make some waves to create and lead new needs is determined by how the company formulates its brand development strategy. But it is best for a branded company to create one special and unique need and continue to lead the development of this need if they want to *be the only one, not just the first one* in the market (this will be discussed in later sections of this chapter).

In a nutshell, when it comes to meeting needs, humans are subjects while products and services are tools that satisfy the needs of the subject. But the reality is instead of focusing on consumers' needs, the purpose of many advertising and marketing strategy is to promote products and services in hopes that they are what consumers want. This is the most obvious myth currently surrounding advertising and marketing.

The Challenges of Meeting Needs

Every company has to deal with *challenges* it faces in the market, which is called *stress* in engineering. Before launching products and services, the company has to propose solutions for stresses they expect to encounter in advance, so they are not in a panic when the problem occurs and let their competitors take advantage of their weaknesses. These stresses can be divided into several categories, including the challenges of environmental change, cultural differences in the way customers operate or use the product, logistics challenges, creation of innovative features, the balance between sales and production, and human assets management. These are the difficulties encountered in business.

Providing products (no matter it is customized or standardized product) that reach the acceptable quality level is one of the habits that exists in the contract manufacturing industry for a long time. But the problem often comes from this lowest acceptable quality level—the product fails once the customer's operation condition is slightly beyond the limits of specifications. There was a company sold mechanical and electrical products to a backward country with a hot climate and poor sanitation. It did not take too long for the product to be damaged in the country. After investigation and analysis, it turned out that the main cause of the damage was that the country was not only too hot but the work environment was not kept clean, so there was too much dust that blocked the vent hole of the product and the original temperature specification was unable to resist this stress.

You may think the poor environmental condition is the buyer's own problem that has nothing to do with the seller. Indeed, but customers never admit their fault; they just turn away and buy other more heat-resistant products. What's worse is the bad reputation has spread by word of mouth since then, and it is all useless no matter how many advertisements they publish and how much clarification they make.

There was a product sold overseas with a stable business, but there were always problems occurred in one country. It was also discovered through long-term investigation that this country had terrible road conditions from the port to the warehouse and the packaging of the product was not strong enough to resist vibration on rough roads. By the time when the product was delivered to the customer, some of the components have been loose already.

The phenomenon of stress is not confined to product but also occurs in service. For example, after a big festival was over, tens of thousands of people wanted to leave at the same time causing the stress on transportation systems. The massive crowd flocked to the MRT station and made the number of people on the escalator and platform exceed their design standards which led to accidents on escalators like entrapment. This is what happens when the stress exceeds the stability limit.

When a special or unexpected problem occurs in a product or a process, there comes the stress. When the problem is not solved in time, customer dissatisfaction is enormously exaggerated and spread out, especially in modern society that information is disseminated rapidly. Therefore, all possible stresses have to be thoroughly thought ahead and be analyzed and planned one by one to make a contingency plan for these stresses.

Be the Only One, Not Just the First One

Fighting over the ranking of market share is pointless. The right focus worthy of attention is the fulfillment of meeting needs.

When you pay attention only to market share, your range of attention is confined to the analysis report about the point of sale, marketing channel, marketing strategy, competitive price, etc. that leaves customer satisfaction behind. Since the chances that customers fully express their satisfaction or dissatisfaction are quite low, the business owner and the marketing department are biased toward the visible data and try desperately to find the answer from it. However, the customer attitude, which is uneasy to collect and analyze, is, as a matter of fact, the most important data, so with the biased theme, the whole company can only make invalid analysis and wasteful investment.

In this case, why does not the company shift its focus from gathering market information and marketing to meeting and creating needs? At the very least, the company can make sure the product they create is unique enough that they do not care if they are ranked in the first place or how to rank high. This goes back to the innovation with the combination of needs and core technology that brings maximum investment benefits.

Needs can be created, motivated, and guided. It depends on whether the proposed new needs are touched people's hearts just like how Steve Jobs made Apple the best in the world by using demand innovation that his achievement still remained peerless. Coca-Cola has been successful for over a hundred years just because its formula is unmatchable, so it does not care too much about whether it is top-ranked, all it has to do is to make sure it is the only one in the market.

Keep focusing on developing and meeting needs in the market. Once you find the key to success, the solution you provide to meet the need becomes your own asset that brings you a flood of sales. This has nothing to do with the rank.

With multiple advancements in research and development tools, management methods, and smart data networks for global marketing, once the product is put on the market, branded company can immediately win customers' hearts and occupy the market in one go, leaving no room for the development of followers or competitors *as long as* they can completely and accurately define needs and apply for patent protection. How can your business survive in the 21st century if you still have the "watch and wait" approach in your mind?

Untold Efforts to Meet the Needs

The first competence of brand performance is *Requirement Development* which refers to the overall requirements in a broad sense that cannot be independently fulfilled by a single department.

In addition to thinking about R&D, manufacturing, and design from consumer needs, for the company that wants to establish a complete brand cycle, it is important to think about suitability, safety, logistics support, reasonable and smooth logistics process, and fast, effective, and cost-effective lifecycle services for products and services. The combination of these aspects requires new thinking and process that are fundamentally different from traditional business administration, so it is going to be a great change for the company.

To truly start from consumer needs, the term "consumer needs" should be broadly defined for it covers all needs through the entire process, not just the needs of end users. It connects the operating environment and the operation method to all the needs during the process from the stage of R&D, then to the stage that delivers the product to the consumer, and finally to the stage that the product is scrapped. If you do not know all these needs, your products or services cannot pass the complete test. Some people may ask, "isn't it outrageous to even count the process of scrapping as a need? " Absolutely not. The Earth is a closed and limited environment with limited resources, hence the scrapped product should be biodegradable with a maximum reuse rate and minimum pollution. The environmental law in many advanced countries is clearly stipulated that export manufacturers have to pay for waste disposal.

There is a wide range of requirements and needs, in addition to consumer needs, there are also requirements of functionality, technique, environmental stress, packaging, logistics, operations and maintenance, repair, improvement and update of technical skills, environmental protection, safety, etc. Before moving on to the stage of innovation and R&D, all requirements should be clearly examined in case that bad quality of design or bad after-sales service caused by negligence may erase other highlights of the innovation and even cause serious trouble for it.

If you still think that marketing is the only way to create performance, there is no way for you to improve your competitiveness!

Local Consumption Culture

Local refers to a wide range of things. For starter, humanity, which includes how civilized the local people are, and this is related to consumers' consumption habits. If you accidentally violate cultural taboos, the failure rate of marketing is absolutely 100%. For example, no one sells pork dishes to Muslims and blood-based foods to Christians. Image is another example. Some images are auspicious symbols in certain regions or ethnic groups while they are ominous symbols in other areas. Apart from these, there are also taboo language, appellation, touching and so on.

The second one is the weather conditions and the environment in the local area, including temperature and humidity; the length of seasons; the air quality, microorganisms, insects, animals, and plants that come with different climate patterns. For example, many outdoor products are intruded by small insects and moisture which greatly accelerates corrosion phenomenon and increases the failure rate of the product. Many analyses of failures of outdoor products reach this very conclusion. It can be said that they are the Kamikaze in nature that attack outdoor products.

The next one is the local laws and regulations which are slightly different in each region even with the same requirements. If the requirement for certification is slightly different from the content, it should be rejected and cause heavy losses.

Target the Right Needs

Many men and women have set a lot of conditions for their future spouse before marriage. After they found the proper person according to these conditions and got married, they realized there were more conditions they did not think of before and felt regretted, but it was too late. Is it easy to define these requirements? Extremely difficult!

Companies that offer manufacturing machinery and equipment face the challenges of technological advancement and the constant improvement of materials, processes, and ordering methods, especially the recent rise of 3D printing, Internet of Things, and Industry 4.0. Manufacturers who purchase these products have to constantly renew them to make sure their quality and speed of manufacturing process keep up with the trend of the times and keep pace with competitors so that they will not be driven out of the market. Hence, companies that provide these devices should put the customers' interests first and find a way to make these devices compatible, scalable, and forward-looking so their customers can maintain their best competitiveness cost-effectively. Instead of stopping at merely providing a product, this raises to the level where they can see the needs of the customer's business development, which in turn makes the customer see them as a long-term business partner.

Modern consumer electronics have so many dazzling features that, however, may only be used less than 30% by ordinary users. Nevertheless, the standard package of these products is always whether the newly released one has more features than the previous one, which is nothing but a waste for both buyers and sellers. If these features can be classified by needs for consumers to select and buy, it can both save costs on production and procurement and make a great contribution to save the earth's resources.

Needs are not only the most important basis for the survival of a company but the first step of all business efforts and the most important objective for all companies. So do your best to research and clearly understand needs before you move on to innovation and R&D!

Be Cautious When Collecting Market Information

There are many types of market sources: phone interview, street interview, mail questionnaire, on-site questionnaire, online questionnaire and so on.

Due to the endless phone scams, people immediately hang up the phone or say they do not have time for an interview if they receive a call from someone they are not familiar with, making it more difficult to get real market data.

Street interviews are also laborious because interviewers often get frustrated with all the refusals they get. However, compared with phone interviews, face-to-face interviews still have certain credibility. People are more willing to confess when they can directly talk to each other face to face and the opinions they express are closer to the real thoughts at the moment.

As the number of Internet users increases, the online survey is also one of the common methods, but unless the users are particularly interested in the topic or the issue is closely related to them, it is often nothing but another click on the "x" in the upper right-hand corner of the screen.

When advertising online or when an online contest asks netizens to choose the champion, there is often the so-called ballot stuffing shows up to manipulate public opinions by hiring a brand marketing consulting firm to take care of it.

That is to say, so far, when it comes to the authenticity of the market survey, there are still many things left to work on or to be made on your own. The fastest way for a company or organization to get real market information is to get direct and authentic opinions from their first-line customers.

The most authentic opinion is often the one expresses dissatisfaction and complaint. After all, criticism is much easier than praise. In this case, you should compare these negative opinions with the pre-listed stresses and the measures for preventing them mentioned earlier in this chapter. After comparing and analyzing it, it should be easy for you to find the problem and the direction of improvement. This process is called "failure reporting, analysis, and corrective action system (FRACAS)." This is a very important database content that can be used as an important tool for the company to develop its product and service strategy.

It Takes Real Effort to Satisfy Customer Experience

Many food manufacturers give away free samples in various supermarkets for experiential marketing to promote their products, but it often produces limited results. There are also many massage chair manufacturers in the department store set up massage chairs for customers to try out, but most people still go away after trying them, so the turnover is not even as high as the one on Father's Day or Mother's Day. This really hurts their feelings, especially the frustration the on-site salesperson feels is not difficult to understand. Although it is cruel, it is indeed a true test that makes them know if the product is good from these customer experiences. What's strange is that these salespeople seldom ask for opinions from these customers as reference for improvement. From this, it is obvious that the manufacturer only cares about whether the customer likes the product, but they do not want to hear anything about improvement.

Frozen foods have been popular since more than twenty years ago and they were claimed to be made by famous chefs. So out of curiosity, I have once ordered one New Year's Eve dinner package. It was so terrible that it ruined the festive atmosphere. Ever since then, I have always kept this type of food at a distance.

Customer experience is the final acceptance of the product. It is a test for the integrity and accuracy of requirements and design, the quality of the manufacturing process, the completeness of the process prepared, suitability, and the thoroughness of the production acceptance process. Comprehensively, it is the strength of the system integration management. If you cannot get a positive customer experience, then the incalculable risks you should take are: how to go back to find the source of the problem? How much does it cost to improve the problem? What are the chances that your customer is willing to tolerate you and trust you again? Therefore, how can't you carefully put all your efforts on customer needs analysis and the system integration management in the first place?

Chapter 4

Innovation and R&D

In the very beginning of this chapter, it is important to emphasize that *requirement development* should be the premise of *innovation and R&D* to prevent resources from wasting when the direction and target are not available.

There are two main directions of innovation: disruptive innovation and subversive innovation. Disruptive innovation disrupts the original structure and function in the entire product range and redesigns it to give it a totally new look. Subversive innovation just keeps the original need and uses a completely different technology to meet this need. In other words, to produce a new product to replace the original one. By definition, this is a revolution for business. No matter what type of innovation it is, what is the most ambivalent feelings investors or business owners have about innovation and R&D? Is it *how many times should I fail? How much does it cost?* Or, *when can we get back the invested money?* One of the favorite questions of smart venture capital firms have for innovation teams is: how many times have you failed? The more it fails, the easier it can gain venture capital's confidence—quite surprising, right? On the other hand, short-sighted venture capital firms ask: how many times have you succeeded? As the saying goes, "failure is the mother of success," it is definitely the more a startup fails, the higher chance of success it has.

In addition to the board of directors' concerns about return on investment (ROI) and payback period, the two major obstacles to innovation and R&D in traditional companies are *standardization* and *quantification*. Management concepts that are generally believed to be beneficial to production are rather toxic to innovation. For this reason, the company should support the development of innovation and R&D in a completely different way from mass production manufacturing and take the following actions :

➤ Develop a positive and active culture of innovation

- ✓ Cultivate an equal culture and eliminate hierarchy in the company
- ✓ Do not negatively criticize yourself or others' ideas or attempts
- ✓ Keep positive thinking, abandon negative emotions
- ✓ Care for employee's physical and mental development and treatment

➤ Create a system of value innovation

- ✓ Redefine value innovation—contribution-oriented
- ✓ Do not establish quantitative performance goals but innovation-oriented goals
- ✓ The innovative leaders themselves should not just be commanders in the innovation team

➤ Innovative operational system

- ✓ An innovative incentive program can produce innovative products
- ✓ Share team information and contributions
- ✓ Focus on the goal of *needs fulfillment*
- ✓ During the innovation process, do not confine yourself to *feature* innovation but take innovation in all aspects into account (Wooden Barrel Theory)
- ✓ Use *contribution value* points rather than market performance as incentive compensation

✓ The administrator thinking, systems, and processes are also innovation targets

Innovation is essentially an experiment. Even if the result of innovation is not as good as expected, it is still a high-value experiment as long as you adopt a positive attitude and get ready to learn. There are at least five things needed to be prepared in advance in pursuit of innovation:

➢ Accept the fact that there are failures in innovation and there is no payback.

➢ Figure out the reasons why the innovation you tried did not work.

➢ Strictly analyze every detail of the innovation to identify the success factors of innovation.

➢ Record the lessons learned in detail and share them with your team.

➢ Try it again (or even start all over again) with the things you have learned.

Once you adhere to the above five elements of innovation, you can significantly increase the chance of success in each innovation process!

Develop the Ability to Interpret Data Correctly

Unless it is the data obtained through experiments, general data sources are multiple scattered that often silently drifting away. Data can be helpful for everything, but if your concept is wrong or the way you treat it is wrong, the collected data is completely worthless and even counterproductive.

What are the types of data collection and application?

1. Weather forecast: disaster prevention

2. Threat assessment: take preventive and defensive measures

3. Market trend: grasp consumer demand

4. Market supply and market demand: transactions and the distribution of various factors

5. Customer satisfaction: products and services suitability, customer relationship management (CRM)

6. Product development trends: improve product technology, functionality, quality, etc.

7. Support and logistics: the smoothness and satisfaction level of logistics services

It is impossible to develop business operations without data, but data has to be effectively organized and interpreted to be transformed into useful information. The key lies in how data demander determines which data should be collected, the purpose and subject they want from data, how the data is collected, how to summarize, organize, and analyze it, how to interpret the results of the analysis, and finally how to use the results of the analysis.

The number of tourists in the night market is increasing day by day. They often only order one portion but occupy the whole table, causing inconvenience for other consumers. This is very important data. Visitors come here for the street food, so naturally, they hope to try a few more different foods; thus, it is the best strategy for them to order only one portion and share it together. There is nothing wrong with this consumption strategy.

So what information can vendors get from this piece of data and how they can respond? For the occupancy problem and the short visiting time problem, they can first adjust the food packaging to make a smaller portion with a lower price so that both sides are happy. Secondly, reduce the number of seats to increase standing capacity so that it can accommodate more customers at the same time without making them feel crowded. Instead of complaining about their consumption habits, you might just as well change your business process and turn the negative effect into a positive one.

The popular big data theory in recent years is a mainstream application of information. Strictly speaking, it is not a new thing, but more like a scientific way to use information. By using data capture methods, paying attention to the authenticity, summarization, timeliness, completeness, and variability of data to observe it, and analyzing the subject, you can get considerable value from it.

Innovation Never Ends

Technology is advancing, the market trend is changing, and competitors have been using different strategies to achieve market leadership. Although it is not recommended for brand management to go with the flow, it has to maintain sensitivity and flexibility to meet market needs, after all, this is the most basic responsibility of branded companies.

The most essential business metric is to meet the needs, including both the needs of active consumers and passive consumers. If it is an active consumer, it is very important to actively interact with them and understand their thoughts because this type of consumer has a mind of their own. Once you are accepted by them, your business is going to prosper and last for a long time. This gives a positive effect on demand and the brand. Once you control or create an endless trend, you are creating and building a brand.

If it is a passive consumer, since it is common consumer psychology that new things are always more attractive than old ones, for this type of consumer, you have to constantly use various packaging and propaganda to stimulate their desire to purchase. This demand creation is more laborious and exhausting. Usually, a traditional company without brand philosophy tends to offer relatively low-priced products and services to passive consumers. Since it is difficult to grasp their needs, it is not easy to control the cost and profit. Besides, the company does not have any classic products that can make them a brand, so they have no choice but to compromise themselves and stick to the type of products they can provide. This is why they have to constantly and laboriously put forward various stimulus programs to boost demand in the market.

There is a saying in the military: "attack is the best form of defense." Innovation is an active attack, whether it is the transformation of a tradition or the creation from nothing. The competition of innovation includes satisfying customers' new needs and surpassing innovations of your competitors. Do not forget to keep an eye on your competitor's strategic direction and process in terms of innovation, otherwise, they may leave you in the dust.

There is NO Rule in Innovation and R&D

Innovation often comes from curiosity and desire for everything. The timing of innovation is unrestricted and unlimited. Sometimes the methods for innovation may even seem stupid and absurd, but it is undeniable that this is how the science, technology, and civilization of mankind progress little by little.

In addition to satisfying curiosity and desire, innovation often comes from meeting the needs or overcoming problems that further leads to new inventions or new discoveries. The important things to ask are: whether innovators are so urgently to feel the needs? Is there any problem that troubles innovators? Is the motivation of innovators strong enough? If these inner conditions are insufficient, they cannot produce any good innovation no matter how good the environmental conditions are.

The environment provided by Google for its R&D teams is enviable. There are entertainment facilities, such as games rooms and gyms, available for team members and exclusive cafeteria for employees and endless snacks. Not only that, the office landscape is remarkable with special environmental features added to the workplace design. But apart from these material incentives, is there any motivation the company can provide to them or to stimulate their creativity?

Some large companies set up R&D departments; set budgets, targets, and deadlines; and then they gather elites to conduct research and development for them, but usually, they wind up failing to achieve satisfactory results within the deadline. What's awkward is that they are wondering if they should continue the project after the failure. How long does it take to be successful? How long can they take the lead after success?

It is undeniable that there have to be fixed resources invested in innovation and R&D, but do not forget sometimes innovation needs the help from your creative muse, not to mention regardless how great the environment is, it is inevitable for the R&D department to feel pressure from the boss. On top of that, since they take up a considerable part of the R&D budget, it blocks other departments from getting support in this regard.

Why not create flexibility first to allow other departments to set up research and development projects? For example, set up a project team that gathers departments like customer service, quality assurance, manufacturing, and logistics; and then make the R&D department have an R&D competition on the same topic with this team. The reason for doing so is that the experience and focus of the two teams are different. One gains experience from the previous products, which makes it creates from the perspective of problem-solving, while the R&D department is more likely to create needs. These two have a different starting point but the goal of innovation is consistent.

Do Not Be Guided by Material Comforts

It is important for innovation to jump out of the rut, otherwise, there is no innovation at all. What is rut? It refers to all existing habits that have built up around someone. The rut was not built in a day, but instead, it starts from the very beginning of your life and everything that happens leaves an imprint on your heart. This is way it is extremely hard to jump out of the rut.

What can be called as rut?

The first rut is a stable state of mind. Stability brings peace and security to people that makes them less likely to take risks. There was a Budai Monk in ancient China who said, "as you transplant rice seedlings in paddy fields so right, you can see the sky in the water ahead so bright; the purification of senses is the natural order to delight, you see, it turns out retreating is advancing in this life." The original meaning of this poem is to encourage people to cultivate their mind and tell them it is better to take a step back when encountering obstacles. By doing so, they can realize that there are more choices around them. However, from the perspective of innovation and R&D, there is never a rich harvest from this paddy field.

The second rut is the organizational structure that determines the status, rights and obligations, the amount of resources, limits of authority, and standard process. It greatly makes people work with stiff minds that everyone in the organization only knows to follow prescribed procedures so that they do not make mistakes and can achieve the biggest goal and the best interest of the organization. Consequently, innovative people inside the organization are not welcome for they are considered as disruptive elements.

If the organization does not quickly adjusts or breaks the rut, there is going to be another bigger challenge coming toward them, that is, the advent of the Internet of Things(IoT). The analysis and decision-making models based on big data are going to replace the current management styles and contents. If the organization does not change, it cannot gain advantages in the era of IoT, thereby lacking international competitiveness.

The third rut is the mindset of payback. Return on investment (ROI) is an investment performance indicator, the most important one in management performance, that is hardly ignored by the board of directors and shareholders. Although they draw up a budget for research and development, they still pay more attention to the ROI and, as a result, fall into a rut of performance expectations. They go back to the concept of "manufacturing" innovation results that still leads them up a blind alley.

So there is a series of questions should be considered: is it really necessary for innovation and R&D to payback its funders? Is it really necessary for the innovation team to be composed of members with high academic degrees and to be led by people at higher levels? Whether the subject and schedule of innovation are strictly determined by the management level or they can be determined by the leader of the team? Is it necessary for all the sources of innovation and R&D to come from inside the company? Can they cooperate with their peers? Is innovation and R&D equal to pouring money down the drain? I cannot provide any answers to these questions because it all depends on the business owner's vision, ambition, resources allocation as well as whether they have the ability to see the big picture.

Do not Forget to Avoid Deadly Risks

Even though it is fine for innovative thinking to be eccentric and unrealistic, when it comes to commoditization, it still has to go back to the basic principle— products and services must *not* cause disasters! No matter how great the innovation can be, if there is a basic deadly element in it, it is ultimately doomed to failure because human safety and health is the top requirement!

The famous cornstarch party in recent years has become popular among young people all over the world, but cornstarch particles can trigger a deadly dust explosion. Based on safety concerns, law-abiding suppliers incorporate anti-explosive materials into cornstarch; however, the fundamentals of dust explosions still remains. It can easily lead to disasters out of carelessness, not to mention if the party hosts do not incorporate explosion-proof materials at all.

Consumer electronics are getting smaller and smaller and they are also getting more and more delicate and closer to users, so the user's risk gets higher as the distance get closer. Skin contact, for example, when the electric power system of the product is abnormal, there is concern about whether the released heat can cause damage to the skin or the material can release toxic substances that pass through the skin. As for the contact to eyes, the designer should consider the safe controllable range and the limit on the length of use for screen brightness. It is the same for ear safety, the control of the sound volume can cause hearing impairment or hearing loss.

There is another one called electromagnetic waves that cause damage to human nerves and brain cells if it is too strong. Since it is difficult for electronics function without using radio waves, the protection from electromagnetic waves gets extremely important. The ability to prevent injury is definitely hidden competitiveness besides functionality. Especially when consumer electronics have become necessities of life in modern society where the total number of users together with the number of both older and younger users increases faster than before, so the importance of safety cannot be overemphasized!

Under extreme weather conditions, the world's food supplies are unstable and there are more food supply projects that emphasize artificial production. For example, genetically modified foods (GM foods), synthetic meat, and health food are all related to the collective health of human beings. GM foods have raised doubts about mutations in both human genes and bacteria in our bodies. The death at a young age of several health food suppliers has also raised consumers' doubts. It has been medically proven that the implantation of stem cells into the human body poses a risk of cancer. Then, if synthetic meat is produced by in vitro cultivation of animal stem cells, does it produce denatured proteins that lead to a disease similar to mad cow disease or produce other toxins? These risks above are all cases that explain why do we need to be concerned about safety during innovation.

Another example is the airbag in cars, although it functions as a protection for the passenger's cervical spine during a collision, for those who wear glasses or contact lens, it may cause blindness when it pops out. When generating new ideas for research and development, you must first thoroughly think about the possible risks. It is especially important to think over the other side of the coin to make sure whether you should move forward or the risks can be completely eliminated. Safety first!

Develop a Innovation Strategy in Accordance with the Target Needs

Although innovation should not be restricted by rut, it does not mean that you can ask for the moon. Before innovation, the only prerequisite is still the direction to meet the needs.

The limit of needs depends on the direction of the company's business strategy or the direction of future transformation. The range of needs can be divided according to global, regional, local, and even customer types. With different types of needs, it can generate a variety of directions. Please refer to *Chapter 3: Requirement Development* for more information.

The main specific needs include the following types:

1. Environmental protection: it can be divided into two categories—energy-saving products (power saving) and pollution prevention products (product materials and packaging).

2. Mobility in aging and care for aging: all kinds of electric and non-electric mobility aids, monitoring and warning equipment.

3. Information and communication technology (ICT): ICT products that serve as primary or support functions. For example, electronics, smart monitoring devices, and command and control (including disaster prevention and relief) products and so on.

4. Food and drug: new technology in animal husbandry and planting; finding and processing new food; new drug development and epidemic prevention measures.

5. Education and entertainment: development of new educational tools, having fun while learning, educational games.

6. Transportation and tourism: combine the intelligent transportation system with business opportunities around logistics, people flow, and sightseeing.

7. Advertising and marketing: combine marketing and shopping with the development of platforms and applications (apps).

8. Financial logistics: the application of combining cash flow with logistics, such as online payment, Internet, IoT.

9. R&D and production tools: corresponding machine tools and software needed for the development trends of IoT, Industry 4.0, and 3D printing technology.

10. Smart building: a new type of building that responds to the multi-functional requirements such as environmental protection, disaster prevention, security, care, etc.

The examples above are just some of the important ones. There are many needs come from much more niche or smaller areas that can be singled out and developed. These needs do not exist alone but are complementary to each other or in the leader-follower relationship.

For example, it requires the use of ICT and advertising and marketing when it comes to the needs for *transportation and tourism*. It requires the use of transportation and production tools when it comes to the needs of *financial logistics*. And for *smart building*, it has to use the technology of environmental protection and aged care as well as ICT.

With the direction of needs and the risks that should be avoided in mind, we can now go all out for innovation and R&D!

Whose Needs Are You Satisfying? Yours or Customers'?

What customer wants is the reason to buy. Whom are you going to convince, the customer or yourself? There is countless innovation in the world, why is it that only less than 1% of innovative products can be accepted? Many innovators have unlimited creativity and always feel that their creativity is so brilliant that it is impeccable. But no matter how good they are in the designer's eyes, the point is whether the original creativity and ideas can win the customers' hearts. We say that humans are sensible beings, and when this is applied in business, it means that you have to touch customers hearts before you can make them buy.

What the customer wants is functionality, but it has different meanings for everyone. Some people like to tell others what they have bought but they do not use it often, so what they bought is actually satisfaction or a chance to brag. Some people are pragmatic and only want to use a few features, so they do not want to pay for the extra features they do not use. There are very few people who both want to buy and want to use all the features. When you design products and services, do you also develop different product strategies for people with different needs?

What the customer wants is ease of use. This involves ergonomics and human factors as well as communication patterns and picture language that create a very different sense of convenience for people of different ages, cultures, and educational backgrounds. For example, when adding new names in an address book, do you store it with an icon or in a list? What does a lightning image represent, battery charging or danger? These subtle differences cause inconvenience when the user has to change their habits. With the advent of the touch panel, many old fashioned people are still accustomed to traditional keyboards with the position and distance different from touch screens. It is said that the reason for Deutsche Bank (DB) mistakenly sent $6 billion to a U.S. bank in October 2015 was a false touch on the touch screen. It is a great challenge to deliver consistent ease of use for all customers.

What the customer wants is the performance, in other words, reliability and maintainability. But when it comes to the choice between long-lasting and short-lived products, it is all about the cost, so customers have different options. The product strategy should consider the stylishness, sustainability, scalability, and substitutability of product. For customers with different needs, there have to be different product levels.

What the customer wants is service. This includes items, content, and prices that are clearly shown, as well as quality and follow-up. What's difficult is that the service receiver is a change factor itself in the process. When the customer is dissatisfied with the service or is unwilling to cooperate, it is difficult to offer services. It is the biggest challenge for service design as well as front-line service providers to figure out how to design service process and content well enough to satisfy customers and maintain service quality.

Taking working in hospitals as an example, an overwhelming amount of interference shows up when patients do not get satisfied and timely treatment. As a result, the standard operating procedure (SOP) in the hospital is not only obeyed by the hospital staff but should be also fully communicated with patients and their families by the first-line medical staff. Every aspect must be designed to make patients feel considerate and reasonable.

There are similar challenges for phone interviewers and service providers in daily life; especially when taking proactive action, the frustration of being rejected is considerable. However, does the customer really want such a service?

Chapter 5

System Safety

Safety is definitely the top priority for running a business, whether it is for internal customers (i.e. employees) or for external customers. How it is possible for employees to work at ease when there is a frequent occurrence of accidents in the company? How it is possible for you to win brand reputation if your products and services frequently cause injuries to people? Due to faulty airbags, Toyota had to recall nine million vehicles worldwide. A cup of scalding hot coffee cost McDonald more than $500,000 in compensation for the customer's injuries. The cost of safety can be so high that it is far beyond our imagination.

When it comes to safety, protecting people from injuries is always the first thing that comes to mind, which includes the protection of employees during the manufacturing process and the protection of customers and users, and then is the protection of facility and property.

There are many types of physical injury, including:

➢ Blast injury

➢ Burns and scalds

➢ Choking on fumes

➢ Blunt trauma, cuts, stab wound

➢ Tripping over, falling off

➢ Crush injury

> Chemical burns caused by strong acids and bases

> Gas poisoning, food poisoning, drug poisoning; etc.

Common causes of injury include:

> Poor product quality or expired product

> Abnormal weather

> Transport accident

> Operational accident

> Unclean environment

> Incomplete or faulty facilities

> Dangerous goods that are not properly controlled

> Hazardous materials or dangerous zone that are not well labeled or well marked

> Electrical accident

> Abnormal monitoring and automatic control accidents; etc.

Normally, we only use the word *safety*, so why do we add *system* in front of it? The causes of hazards are by no means accidental, but a series of omissions being mutually affected and deteriorated that eventually leads to an accident that threatens the safety of individuals. The international community has taken a series of steps to establish a safety management system so as to prevent accidents from happening:

> Develop a safety policy,

> Safety plan and target setting,

> Set up a security organization,

> Safety analysis and risk assessment,

> Establish and design security mechanisms,

- ➤ Implementation arrangements,

- ➤ Acceptance testing,

- ➤ Certification and accreditation of the system

- ➤ Regular and irregular disaster prevention drills

This whole process builds a complete safety system, so internationally it is called *System Safety*.

Safety is indeed a serious matter that involves business reputation, insurance claim, market trust, asset loss, and in some serious cases, it is a matter of life and death for the company. This is why governments around the world, as well as insurance and reinsurance industries, put all efforts to develop management and technical standards regarding system safety, hoping that companies can do their best to promote it.

The range of safety-related issues in business varies greatly from attribute to attribute, so the practice is also different from one another. For a small export product, it only requires to perform the risk analysis, prove it is safe (test report), and then apply for safety certification. As for large electromechanical products and facilities, they are subject to design review, construction supervision, trial run, and the safety regulatory approval of the local government where these products and facilities are installed. But in fact, the most important part is the operating unit, such as various factories, airports, docks, stations, hotels, restaurants, cinemas, shopping malls, hospitals, and office and residential buildings, where various facilities and equipment coexist in the same site that makes it an important concern for system safety.

Since it is called system safety, let's take a look at a hypothetical model that shows what happens when there are system safety loopholes:

There is a union station where the tracks and facilities are shared by three separate railway companies in a big city. One day, during regular work hours, there was suddenly an announcement saying: "your attention, please. A fire emergency has been reported in the station, please evacuate immediately." However, due to a lack of precise and prudent SOP and a lack of opportunity for live emergency response drills, when driven by panic, there was a mass of people taking off running toward the exit of the station like crazy. Under such a situation, there were fewer people burnt to death or choked to death on the fumes while there were more people pushed down and trampled to death in the stampede. This can be the result of a lack of an overall safety system for emergency and disaster response!

Companies should consider all possible situations that may happen when customers use their products and services and think about how to establish the ability to strengthen system safety within the company from the perspective of culture, organization, process, education and training, and disaster risk reduction.

A Bad Safety Record is Like Burn Scars

It has been over ten years since the 2008 Chinese milk scandal, the incident of melamine-tainted milk powder. Up to now, people from China are still purchasing baby milk powder when traveling abroad, which has astonished many countries in the world. So you can see how hard it is to erase the impression of having a bad safety record from people's hearts.

Taiwan is world-famous for its street food, but after some food safety incidents like plasticizer incident, toxic starch, and fake oil crisis, every housewife now buys food with the most meticulous care, checking for the right brands and labels. Vendors at food stalls also post announcements saying that it is by no means toxic ingredients in their food. It takes more than ten years to build a brand, but when it comes to destroying a brand, it only takes one day!

We learn and grow from every first-time experience, which is always our most profound impression, and the accumulation of these experiences can be deeply and eternally engraved on our minds. It is especially uneasy to forget shared experience among the public. It is like a child wants to play with fire—if they are accidentally burned once, it takes a long time before they dare to try it again and this time they do it with great carefulness.

This kind of memory affects the subsequent behavior and causes a chain reaction, which goes viral between consumers, especially in modern society with so much developed social media. In the olden days, people use the saying "bad news has wings" to describe bad news can spread thousands of miles, but now, they travel far more than a thousand miles. With the click of a mouse, news can just spread ten thousands of miles in the twinkling of an eye.

"The number of customers has decreased significantly from 2014 to 2015 due to the food safety scandal which foreign objects were found in food. McDonald's Japan was going to step up its efforts to improve its performance by laying off employees," according to Japanese media reports. "Meanwhile, it announced the consolidated earnings forecast for the fiscal year 2015 (from January 1, 2015 to December 31, 2015) saying that they expected a net loss of 38 billion yen (approximately $340 million), which has been increased compared with that of 21.8 billion yen (approximately $195 million) in the previous fiscal year, so the company imposed measures such as layoffs, hoping to turn losses into profit in the next fiscal year."

It is not just food industry that has safety concerns, there are also safety incidents, such as plane crashes, gas explosions, dust explosions, traffic accidents, that happen in other industries. A safety scandal of a company is equivalent to a scar marked with a red-hot iron that can never be erased because the media always records every detail of the event permanently for free.

Safety is Always the Top Priority

In terms of product supply, countries around the world have developed various safety regulations and certification systems to substantively protect consumer's personal safety and their basic human rights. This is also the basic threshold for exporting products to the international market.

Companies in many advanced countries are generally promoting a "Zero Harm" campaign. The purpose of this campaign is to focus on the values of human life and family ties, not business interests. The spirit of this campaign is that every employee has to raise their family, which can refer to parents, wives and children or even siblings, so once there is an accident or disaster occurs, it is not just the personal loss of the employee, but the loss of a family. Additionally, once a safety incident occurs in the company, it also leaves a sad memory that takes a long time to heal inside the company that haunts other employees and affects their mood in the workplace.

Besides human life, safety is closely related to society and country as well. For example, individually, information security involves leakage of personal information and fraud cases; commercially, it affects corporate confidentiality and business interests; as for national defense, it can lead to a national crisis for the country. The consequences of these events are very unbearable for those who are involved.

Food security affects the nation and the next generation. It is safe to say that the destruction of the quality of life and work and the national health insurance system can lead to more serious consequences and impacts than financial loss. Poor quality food has the potential to harm every consumer in the country, which make it an invisible killer who murders the competitiveness of the country.

As for epidemic prevention, when the disease is out of control, besides the fact that the number of deaths is immeasurable, all economic activities in the country go into an economic ice age and the consumption falls to the lowest level like the whole society is controlled by an invisible ghost that can easily destroy the country.

Get the First-hand Information All the Time

Normally, there are at least three levels in a traditional organizational structure that generate the division of labor with each level is solely responsible for its own duties. Under normal circumstances, this functions well without causing problems, but when a major disaster occurs, it away requires the highest-level executives to explain to the public, to give commands, to deal with the problem, or to handle the aftermath and find out who should be held accountable for it.

Every time I see this situation, I cannot help but worry about these highest-level executives. How many safety-related details and preparations do they really know? How many owners of public or private companies really see safety as the highest goal of business operations and care about it personally? There is always a "more important" thing in business for them to be busy with, so we can often see in the media that when a major safety incident occurs, for the irresponsible senior executives, there are usually three types of attitudes: the first one is to refuse to show up, but choose a spokesperson on their behalf to deal with the media; the second one is to show up with a puzzled look because sometimes they do not even know what the problem is and can only talk in circles. The last one is to make promises in person saying they are definitely going to improve or deal with the situation, but the problem is not necessarily improved later. All these three types only add insult to injury for the brand after the safety incident occurs.

Passing the Buck Does Not Make the Accident Disappear

On the one hand, you want to make more money and earn more profit; on the other hand, you refuse to accept obligation and take responsibility. So in the event of an emergency, your first reaction is always to quickly deny the responsibility by saying: "it is none of my business!"

In 2016, there were several phone battery explosions occurred on Samsung's mobile phones which posed a direct threat to the user's personal safety. Generally, the first instant reaction was thinking: "they must use some non-original chargers." And then: "maybe the quality of the outsourced batteries was poor." It was not until a few days later that the company announced it would take full responsibility. Out of a sudden, this type of mobile phone was immediately pulled off the shelves worldwide and the sold ones were also banned from aircraft. The direct and indirect losses of the accident have reached billions of dollars. At the time when the accident was not investigated clearly yet, people chose to take the most careless and negligent attitude to deal with it. You had to push them so hard to make them dig deeper. Eventually, there were explosions occurred around the world that fueled global customers' rage, and it was until then did they finally take responsibility. From this case, we see that people are inclined to avoid troubles and responsibility in the event of an accident and see how serious the disaster such human nature can cause.

An accident is locked in the Pandora's box, each password on the lock of the box is like an omission. When the passwords match (omissions happen at the same time), it opens the box and releases the accident.

Rigid Rules are the Biggest Risks

We often hear the term standard operating procedure (SOP) in many industries as if everything can be done with it, but actually it is not. The SOP is applicable to a process that is recurring, repetitive, and stable. It is not the universal solution because there are always exceptions. Accidents are often caused by these exceptions that the company has to use the corporate culture and even society's common values to deal with them. If the company overemphasizes SOP and formulates principles for handling circumstances under which the SOP is not applicable, then employees just stubbornly stick to it without having their own thoughts and cause major disasters.

There was a classic example. In a New York subway station, a Korean man was pushed on subway tracks and killed by the train. On the next day, the *New York Post* published the photo showing he was catching hold of the platform edge moments before death on the front page and titled "Doomed." Controversy in media ethics aroused immediately after the publication and so did the reflection of why there is no one around to help him. Some netizens lamented that the whole thing was "using sensory stimulation to replace real news" and it was downright brutal.

For this newspaper photographer, this was nothing more than another subject for news and he just followed the SOP as a photographer. But the fault is not in the SOP itself but in the misunderstanding and misuse of it. Here, the misunderstanding part is he neglected that there are something far more important than SOP that should be identified as the top priority—human values.

It is just as the Chinese proverb goes, "gold cannot be pure, and people cannot be perfect," so it is important to pre-set principles for situations that are not covered by the SOP.

Small Changes Can Bring Big Results

From products to systems—whether it is purely mechanical, purely electronic, or electromechanical—they all include elements like functionality, input and output signal, monitoring and surveillance, control, protection, operations and maintenance, and human interface. Under normal operation, they can both perform duties alone and work together. But when operating abnormally, they are harmful and greatly affect each other.

What is "small changes can bring big results"? When one of the elements is abnormal, it gradually affects all the other elements that leads to the collapse of the whole system in the end and even brings disasters.

Ask the questions below and write them down. Let's start with the environment. What does the environment where the system is located look like? Is there any natural disaster? How often is it? How serious they can be? And what harm does it cause to the people and property inside or around the system?

As for operation, is there any problem, such as pushing, the disappearance or error of signal, power loss, brake failure, interval error, overload, falling down, on fire, heavy fumes, and emergency rescue, occurs during the process? What are the chances of them happening? How serious they can be? And what harm does it cause to the people and property inside or around the system?

The third one is the product or the system itself. Is it possible for their functionality to cause any danger to people, such as collision, running over, high heat, radiation, explosion, pinch, burns, bright light, loud noise, dust, poison, and fumes? What are the chances of them happening? How serious they can be? Under what kinds of circumstances do these accidents occur? And what harm does it cause to the people and property inside or around the system?

Do parts of the product or system interfere with each other? For example, motion of machine parts, the impact of high temperature, friction, electromagnetic interference, signal range, expansion and contraction, and human-machine interface. What happens when these interfaces are not well-defined? What are the fault symptoms? What are the consequences?

If any problem occurs in any of these four levels, it affects and spreads among other levels and causes greater and bigger problems. Therefore, it is important to discuss these safety issues from the top down or from the bottom up at the same time to compare whether there is any negligence or omission, and then take measures to avoid and prevent them from occurring.

Chapter 6

Quality Management

When it comes to quality, no one can get the point with an "edge ball"!

Theoretically, quality plays a very critical role in the company for it represents discipline and productivity. The problem is that no one wants to be criticized, especially if their promotion and rewards are closely related to this, so it makes everyone avoid *quality* like the plague.

For example, the quality performance of R&D can be overshadowed by senior executives' expectations for innovation. Business operators are eager to launch new products into the market to compete with their competitors, so they shorten the complete process of quality verification. Or, the quality performance is concealed so as to save costs and achieve production target in the manufacturing process.

Over time, quality is diminished! Even the business owner is not willing to take responsibility for the quality incident. Instead, in order to pursue short-term profits, they are standing on the opposite side of quality and even makes quality control personnel find themselves redundant and unwanted. Companies in pursuit of brand building should be more careful about this.

Quality is a key factor in international trade. For this reason, the International Organization for Standardization (ISO) standardizes the quality management system and develops the ISO 9000 series of quality standards, which has been implemented internationally for more than 20 years. However, with the generalization of the quality management system, there have been many standards ambiguously interpreted and misused. These standards are just copied word for word with the most superficial knowledge of the system, losing the purpose and key concepts of quality management.

Another common problem is that quality assurance can only do things right, but cannot do the right thing. Some companies are reluctant to invest enough money in quality, so the defect of the product is concealed under unrealistic statistics. Out of reluctance, they do not invest sufficient resources to fully carry out tests and evaluations that enable the product to be used in various environmental conditions, so they secretly shorten the testing schedule or reduce the number of testing samples.

The achievement of quality can be seen from two aspects. The first one is from a broad sense, that is, the general rules for ISO. The entire business operations of the company are included in quality management, for example, personnel, finance, business management, marketing, product design, manufacturing, logistics, and customer service, nothing is excluded.

The key practice is that the business owner should take the lead, bring all the company's activities in this practice, and take the smallest details into account. In such a corporate culture, even the physical and mental conditions of employees are contained in this ultimate quality management, so much so that employees feel they are suffocating.

The second aspect of quality is from a narrow sense, that is, the quality control of products, especially the design and manufacturing processes that are extremely meticulous. For example, the application of Six Sigma (6σ) which only allow defects per million opportunities (DPMO) in raw material inspection, production process inspection, outgoing quality control (OQC) and so on. If this kind of exquisite quality control does not act in concert with the after-sales survey, then it makes the whole meaning of quality control before leaving the factory blurred. In this case, quality assurance officers have to struggle with invisible statistics every day that sacrifice their quality of life as well as their relationship with family.

Generally speaking, a company that adopts a broad sense of quality also includes the practices of a narrow sense of quality which makes all staff of the company lives in abysmal conditions. On the other hand, in a company that only adopts a narrow sense of quality, its employees are drowning in work while officials have nothing better to do at work.

To establish a quality culture that is both efficient and in line with human nature, my observations and suggestions are as follows:

➢ Make sure that the level of quality assurance should be above the level of development and operations in the organization.

➢ Quality should be carried out from the top down that starts from the establishment of quality culture. The highest-level executives of the company must declare and take concrete actions to foster a comprehensive quality culture.

➢ Truth is the cornerstone of quality assurance. All quality-related actions must be taken in accordance with truths. So it is important to regard presenting truth as the biggest goal—from the needs of customers to every process of raw materials, research and development, production, and logistics.

➢ When defects are discovered, the department that goes through the process at that very moment should temporarily take responsibility for bad quality and deal with it immediately. They should use the root cause analysis (RCA) to find the root cause and the accountability later, and then improve it systematically.

The responsibility for quality assurance should only remain at the top-level management to implement the formulation, supervision, and inspection of goals and policies. Quality control should be allocated to each department and allow employees to conduct autonomous management. As for the quality engineering, a group of professionals in quality analysis and management should be established to control quality assets, such as quality management tools, techniques, statistical analysis, inspection and testing, failure analysis, etc., and adopt methods like professional concentration and project support to send the quality responsibility back to the responsible department, so there is no buck-passing and everyone is the bearer of quality.

Maintaining Competitiveness with High Quality

It only meets the lowest requirement when making a product that meets the specification. But when trying to break into the market, you have to encounter many more challenges from different stresses and the most realistic tests. If you want to be invincible in the market, you have to make a product that carries something far beyond specification requirements to satisfy customers from different cultures and regions.

The manufacturing industry is the lifeblood of a country's economy. It has to pass specific laws and regulations of the local country when exporting goods abroad. Many managers spend money to pass these regulations to get their goods exported successfully as expected, but since they all share a money-saving mindset, it is quite questionable whether they do their best to make their products perfect. Naturally, such competitiveness lacks a solid foundation.

Another myth is that turnover is somehow in contradiction with quality which means the greater the turnover they get, the lower the quality they want to provide. This is reminiscent of the story about a porter who won the lottery told by Dr. Sun Yat-Sen, the father of the Republic of China. The porter hid the lottery ticket in his bamboo pole; however, out of joy and excitement, he thought now that he was rich, he did not need to make his living with this stinky pole anymore, so he threw the pole away, but it did not occur to him that his lottery ticket was thrown away as well. After gaining popularity in the market, the company that throws away its original quality, the reason that makes it popular and prosperous, is just like the porter who threw away his stinky pole. In the end, they lost everything that establishes the foundation of their hard work.

No matter how popular you are, you must not even slightly reduce the quality of your products and services, otherwise, it is only a matter of moments before your customers turn their back on you and leave you for good.

Quality is a Promise

The core of traditional business philosophy is profit maximization and its highest ethical standard is profit making, so they tend to think it is a bad thing to spend more money and it is a good thing to save money, not to mention what you mostly hear from quality is bad news. It is like you are spending a lot of money in return for punishment and suffering.

This is why when it comes to layoffs, quality assurance officers is the first one down; when it comes to saving money, the quality assurance budget is the first one down; and whenever there is a problem with the product or service, quality assurance is again the first one to be held responsible for it. They are not only scolded severely by customers in the front line but also the first one to be blamed in the company. In this case, no wonder they have to continuously switch companies like "orphans" who can only settle down when they find a company that takes quality seriously. What a helpless career for them! We often think that *quality* is born after the Industrial Revolution of the 19th century, but actually, it goes way back to the time when ancient China built the Great Wall and the Egyptians built the pyramids. There was even detailed specifications recorded in the Bible when the Temples were built. All of these were the quality requirements in manufacturing and they were also promises that were made by the workers to show their determination to accomplish these tasks. The only difference is that these were promises to the emperor and God, not to customers.

Therefore, in the modern era when quality becomes a part of business, the promise is made to the buyer, who, however, has no power over the seller, so the quality can be reduced without being punished by a greater power. Quality is the basic responsibility of the company to consumers that is both a presence of conscience and a promise to the market. They cannot avoid or deny the responsibility as much as possible just because the pressure of being beheaded is no longer exists. "品質 (pronunciation: pin zhi)" means quality in Chinese. Besides the meaning of "品" mentioned in *Chapter 1*, here it means comments get from many people. "質(zhi)" is the quality of products and services. Together, they mean "the comments given by the public are the real quality of products and services." The pre-shipment inspection or other external accreditation is for reference only.

Vague and Superficial Data Covers up the Truth

Products from the assembly line have been shipped out of the factory and they have passed various tests and have been certified for export. However, when they are launched into the market, there come problems immediately, or in a month, or in three months, or in half a year... So what happened to those proofs of passing so many inspections in the first place? What is the effectiveness of those export certificates? Do you really think they have any substantial effect when you just go through the motions?

No matter what data you acquire before the product leaves the factory, it can only be used as a reference—you cannot take it seriously. Any man-made efforts cannot really resist the various environmental stresses imposed on the products. There should be scarcely any business owner who can sit back and relax but still get their way by controlling and using all kinds of data. What's really happening is they often receive unexpected warnings from the market.

For those contract manufacturers who are one of the suppliers for a global brand system, this should sound familiar: every now and then, you receive notification of defects from the quality assurance department of the brand vendor. Senior executives in your company then have to immediately visit the brand vendor to explain the problem and make an instant improvement. This situation shows that there are still defects in components produced by contract manufacturers, and they have even already gone through numerous inspections and countless quality control processes required by the branded company.

Why is the quality of the product before leaving the factory is discounted after launching into the market? Most of the pre-shipment inspections check quality specifications under a single stress at a time, such as temperature cycle, humidity cycle, vibration cycle, sealing pressure, etc. However, in reality, when they are sent to the market, they have to go through stresses that come from the whole environment, so the conditions (including packaging, transportation, and storage) are influenced by these irregular and complex stresses that are barely able to be replicated in factories or laboratories, but can only rely on market experience. In this case, it is important to pay more attention to market data than inspection data.

The reason why the company's competitiveness falls behind is greatly related to this incomplete understanding. When the quality of the product meets the specification, you just pass it by the skin of your teeth. So do not be so smug!

Every Mistake is Equally Huge for a Serious Accident

In 1986, when NASA launched the Space Shuttle Challenger, it, unfortunately, exploded and killed everyone in it. After a 32-month investigation, they found the accident was caused by a failure in an O-ring that sealed the joint, a small part that just cost tens of dollars, yet it led to a loss of more than $4 billion space shuttle and six invaluable astronauts. Every mistake is equally terrible!

During the flight, it should constantly indicate remaining fuel quantity in the fuel tanks and the pilot's judgments depend on this small fuel probe. If it fails and the message received is wrong, then the aircraft may crash when running out of fuel.

If the vent hole of a machine is in the wrong size, it reduces the efficiency of heat dissipation and gradually lowers the quality of the machine. If it is sold abroad, the reputation of the company is going to be reduced and its competitiveness may even vanish like a puff of smoke. Every product in the hands of customers is a representative of the company's brand.

These examples above simply explain why every mistake is equally huge with the potential for serious consequences. Thus, from this point of view, it makes sense why quality is the basis of the brand. When the first emperor of the Han dynasty in ancient China, Emperor Gaozu of Han (Liu Bang), was in critical condition, he encouraged the crown prince by saying: "do not fail to commit an act of kindness just because it is small in scale; do not commit an act of evil just because it is small in scale," which unexpectedly travels through time and space to point out the basic spirit of quality today. Only when people do every small thing practically and correctly can they accomplish the big thing.

Find the Right Cure

The manufacturing industry relies on the Eight Disciplines (8D) to resolve problems with quality control. When there is an error, this problem-solving process finds the root cause, takes action to eliminate the root cause, and then implements permanent countermeasures. It can also identify why the system allows this error to occur. Preventive measures can also identify why errors above occur in the management system and prevent recurrence.

However, if the quality culture of a company is similar to the one described in the previous sections, then it is already difficult for them to put efforts into finding out the cause of the problem. Since various departments are so used to buck-passing, the quality assurance officers have to run off their feet between these departments and solve a problem without knowing the root cause.

The first and the biggest difficulty is it greatly relies on evidence to find out the cause of the problem, but the questions are: do they still retain all pieces of evidence collected when the error was discovered? Are these pieces of evidence complete and correct? Have they have been correctly defined, classified, and formatted in advance? In this definition, whether it has already clarified and assigned the responsibility? With this preliminary planning, now you have a chance to find out the cause of the problem.

"Failure Mode and Effect Analysis (FMEA)" is the way to detect the problem in advance, which is a source of problem prevention for the forward-thinking design. Although almost all professionals in quality assurance know this tool, most of them cannot implement it correctly. One of the reasons is that there have to be sufficient reasons for failure mode to be confirmed in advance. Even if a company engages in the R&D and production of specialty products, it rarely creates an experience database to provide complete and correct data sources. Another reason is that in order to know if these failure modes have been successfully prevented by designers, it requires stress screening tests during the process, which takes a lot of time and money. On top of that, it is usually not welcomed by all the other departments, especially by boss and business department.

In this case, when the source of the problem is not defined, designed, and verified in advance; and the cause cannot be fully confirmed after the problem occurs, an 8D report is just a tool the quality department use to justify themselves. When the problem occurs again next time, they have to make another case for it and try to justify themselves again. The problem is never solved and the quality department is continuously left holding the bag.

Is this situation really unsolvable? Of course not. In addition to the widely known FMEA in the manufacturing industry, there is a system called "Failure Reporting, Analysis, and Corrective Action System (FRACAS)," which aims to define, classify, collect, analyze, assign responsibility, and draw up improvement plan for problems with products and services occurring in the market. Then, it conducts market verification and connects with FMEA to compare with each other and revises. In this way, it establishes a closed-loop system for sustainable improvement. This system is not well known, but it has been applied to a few large scale projects and has already achieved results.

The 8D report is not useless, but it has to be based on the pragmatic interconnection and interaction between the FMEA (R&D and production) and the FRACAS (customer experience) to achieve true quality improvement.

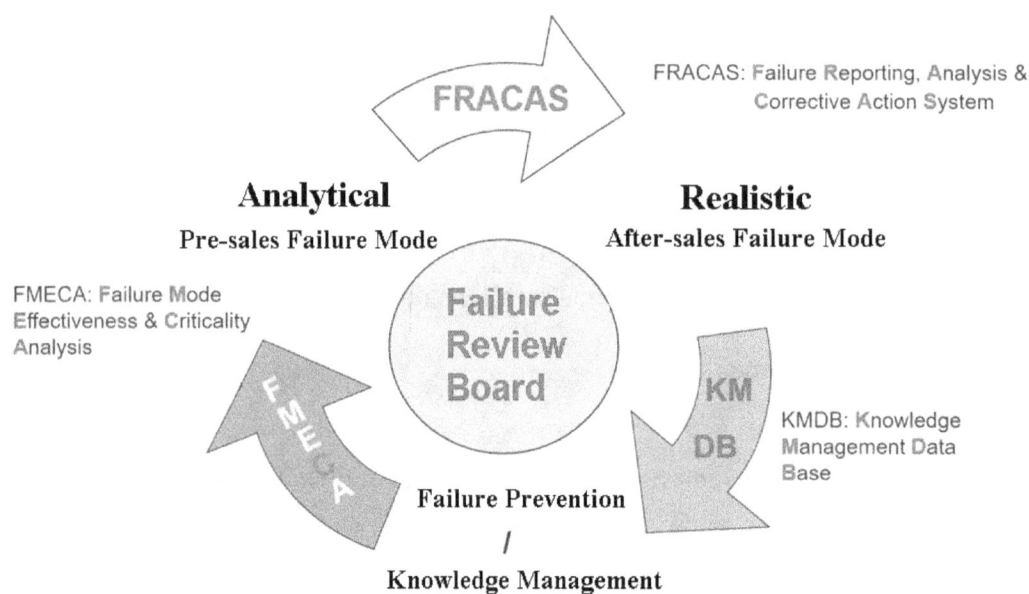

The relationship between FMEA and FRACAS

Haste Makes Waste

Those who have worked with teams from technologically advanced countries must have gotten an impression from their engineers of being very careful of rules and being slow in thinking and moving as if they are not very active. But is this the truth?

They want to take their time to think thoroughly before making a decision—this is why they think slow. They want to cautiously confirm every step is accurate enough to be done right the first time—this is why they move slow. Being slow in thinking and moving saves more time and money than being thoughtless and impetuous that causes more problems or even leads them to go back to square one. You know what they say: haste makes waste.

There is another more important support behind them that is called the knowledge database. A knowledge database with rich information sources is compiled into general standards that can be national, regional, or global. If it is the company's exclusive experience data, then it is built in the corporate headquarters and shared inside the company. So when the seemingly dorky foreign engineers encounter difficulties in their work, all they have to do is to go back to the company's internal website to get backend support, unlike our engineers who have to rack their brains and burn the midnight oil to solve the problem.

The powerful knowledge database has made science, technology, and management develop faster and faster while the backwardness has been left farther and farther behind. When doing research or making a decision, it seems that we are all starting from zero which makes people hang back out of fear and over-cautiousness while there are people who can rely on the experience database to easily start from one hundred and move forward to reach two hundred. This is the Matthew Effect.

" For whosoever hath, to him shall be given, and he shall have more abundance; but whosoever hath not, from him shall be taken away even that he hath." — Matthew 13:12, KJV.

There is a similar situation called "follow the precedent" we often hear in politics or in the workplace. In the absence of any precedent, there are more risks and responsibilities to take for a proposal and the chance of being approved by the government scarce to none that affects countless opportunities for innovation. Such loss is significant yet immeasurable for the country because both creativity and opportunity are unfortunately stillborn.

If you do not want your competitiveness to be reset to zero at any time, you have to organize your experience into knowledge systematically and then turn the knowledge into norms and standards. If they are inadequate and flawed, it is definitely impossible for you to gather the collective strength and compete with international competitors.

It is Better to Scratch Back on Your Own

In the mindset of seeking cheap and cheerful deals, the company is certainly trying to bring down the price when outsourcing. But what does it take to make the contract manufacturer take quality into consideration? Under such small budget with nearly no profit to be made, they naturally try to save costs as much as possible, especially labor costs, since material specifications and procurement costs are unable to be changed flexibly. When working in intolerable conditions of being exploited, employees are not only in no mood to work but may even prepare for a job change at any time. In this case, how is it possible for them to produce products with good quality?

Contract manufacturers that have long been working with international factories are accustomed to using cheap and cheerful as a competitive strategy. So when they have products or semi-finished products that require outsourcing, they also want it to be cheap and cheerful. In this way, the entire supply chain from the upstream to the downstream gets sucked into the poverty vortex and sinks down together, as a result, their product quality is naturally never improved and is unable to reach the same level as the product quality produced by international brand vendors.

A new era of manufacturing has been coming on strong. New modes of production introduced by 3D printing technology, Internet of Things, and Industry 4.0 are pushing forward customization. The old and previous ones are unable to adapt to this new era, which not only breaks the supply chain but the finished product manufacturers are also going to be eliminated from the market if they fail to fully update their technology and production tools.

In addition to the manufacturing revolution in modes of production, the traditional concept of quality management is almost certain to be unsuitable in the 21st century. Besides maintaining the requirements of fast delivery, *flexibility* and *modularity* in new modes of production are the two key points to adapt to customized requirements. Product suppliers must re-plan and transform the traditional product structure into module formats as soon as possible and adjust the quality management methods accordingly.

What modularity and flexibility require is a large amount of customer demand data which must be classified as different types of products that are closest to different types of customers to establish a competitive basis for rapid supply. On this basis, finished product manufacturers should possess sufficient technical analysis capability to convert customer needs into technical specifications and allocate them to each module of the product (i.e. the functionality and technical specification requirements of each module). Finally, they have to formulate the quality requirements and set out acceptance conditions for these requirements of each module.

Do not Leave any Mistake Uncorrected

As mentioned in the previous two sections, the commonly used FMEA tool does not seem to be substantially effective. One of the reasons is that there is a lack of knowledge base which is due to the fact that we are not used to or able to use accumulated market experience to build one. Another reason is the psychological factor. We do not list failure modes for fear that we might fail to solve them, so we might as well do not list them at all!

Many years ago, I have participated in a multinational project and was responsible for the quality of parts and components in the first-line. One day, I found one of the parts did not meet the quality requirements, so I asked for rejection in the project management meeting. Surprisingly and unexpectedly, the Chairman said this part was one of the parts that comprised the equipment that must be shipped back to Taiwan as soon as possible to combine with other equipment and to conduct the integration testing. In this case, there should be no quality problem. The point was this "no quality problem"—instead of asking the equipment supplier to improve and then re-submit it—what he meant was that I could not point out any problem that would interrupt the schedule and prevent the equipment from being shipped back to Taiwan on time. Eventually, I managed to make senior executives have another meeting, and after discussing, they agreed to temporarily use the equipment with the defective parts and asked the supplier to improve it within the given deadline. This case shows the attitude we have whenever there is a problem, instead of eliminating it like destroying an arch enemy, we are so used to conceal and bury the problem.

Another attitude is about how we see the standard specifications. For product manufacturers, the most time-saving, trouble-saving, and cost-effective thing is the manufacturing of a single standard product with economic batch quantity. But if the product is marketed all over the world, the scope of the standard should be broad enough to accommodate different markets, such as different geographic market area. Now here comes the challenge: in order to adapt to the temperature range from the Arctic to the tropics, it requires the use of parts and materials that are good enough to meet the quality requirements, so the cost would be high, which, however, contradicts with the goal of cost saving.

So when designing, failure modes under extreme weather conditions are compromised and concealed; hence, the manufacturer is taking the gamble when launching this product, hoping that this specification is able to adapt to the extreme climate. Additionally, they like to take a chance on whether the consumer will tolerate the failure. For them, if they pass, they win. But what if they fail? Well, it just another modification at most.

No matter what reason that makes failure modes unable to be faithfully presented and even be prevented in the design stage, these failures become unexploded bombs walking around in the market that no one can prevent them. They may take away the reputation and profit of the company all of a sudden.

Do not Let Problems Wander in the Organization

It is in our nature to pursue good fortune and avoid disaster, but it is not a good thing when this happens in the organization. *Problem* is always unpopular, which is why everyone avoids it like the plague when there is a problem or a foreseeable problem is coming their way soon. When this happens, there are people pretend they cannot see it; there are people cleverly dodge it; there are people repack it and then send it to someone else; there are people conceal it; however, there is no one willing to solve it.

The reality is that the problem does not go away on its own. It is like a piece of garbage which, no matter where you hide it, slowly rots and stinks, and there is no one there to offer you waste management service to help you get rid of it. You have to clean it yourself.

The best strategy for problem-solving is do not let the problem occur in the first place, but it is easier said than done. When a problem with products and services occurs in the market, it is usually the customer service that handles the customer complaint. If they cannot handle it, the problem should be sent back to the quality department for analysis and improvement. The difficulty of problem-solving starts here.

The first problem is whether the quality department has detailed enough data. For example, does the customer clearly express their dissatisfaction? What is the situation at that time? What is the actual situation of the product or service? Does the same problem occur again and again? What is the customer's background?

The next problem is the internal organizational challenge in the company which is more complicated. First, analyze and classify all problems that can be thought of in advance and identify who is responsible for the problem. Next, let the person responsible take precautions from institutional and design aspects, then develop standard norms or processes. Once there is a problem presented to the quality department, they need to analyze it and turn it to the person responsible to complete the improvement from these two aspects.

There are two types of *problems* wandering in the organization. The first one is the pre-analysis and prevention of the problem. Is the relevant person responsible willing to accept these assigned problems and do everything in their power to take preventive measures? If no one comes forward to admit responsibility for the problem, then there is no one held responsible for it and prevents it from happening.

The second type of wandering problem is when a problem comes, is the analysis and responsibility the quality department made and assigned convincing enough for the top management of the company and the person responsible? If the answer is no, then there is no way to find the right person responsible for it, leaving it unsolved forever that turns into a nightmare the quality department cannot shake off.

Is the problem caused by the quality department? Of course not, but the quality department is responsible for the prevention and management of the problem. The company is full of problems like a landfill with scattered garbage everywhere that undermines its development unless it can establish an actual quality management culture.

Procedure Must be Transparent

It is inevitable for various departments to start the internal competition for the achievement of their respective performance targets. If good business strategy and management is unavailable in the company, there is going to be an imbalance or even conflict in performance. On top of that, company's strategy is often influenced by business directions, such as heavy on production, light on quality; heavy on sales, light on R&D; and heavy on R&D, light on services, which make departments go against each other that basically wastes resources on a pointless competition.

That is why modern management puts emphasis on SOP. Only SOP can establish the fundamental rules of corporate behaviors, balance the company's internal conflicts, and put all resources and strength of the company on business objectives.

As for the question of how to formulate the SOP to achieve the maximum effect, first, it requires to set an overall goal as the source for the SOP, and then make it properly flow through various departments according to the implemented strategy, including its primary functions, secondary functions, and supporting functions. At the same time, it should take the corresponding relevance and sequence order of different functional departments into account to generate corresponding relations between supply and demand within the company. Last, put these relations in the SOP, define the interface, and establish respective goals and objectives.

The integrity, correctness, and executability of SOP is another important point besides the specialty product of the company. If the specialty product is the skeleton, then the SOP is the ligament and cartilage. Without them, the movement of the skeleton is quite stiff and even tangled.

Judge Correctly Before Dealing with the Problem

In the 9/11 attacks in 2001, after the two buildings of the World Trade Center were hit one after another by planes, firefighters were immediately dispatched and worked separately to arrange equipment for firefighting and rescue and to handle the crowd evacuation. However, unexpectedly, the heat of the flame melted the steel beams of the building, causing the building to collapse completely and kill all people inside. This case is the first time ever in the world of course, so there is no precedent to follow at all. However, the beginning and the end of the event indicate that it can lead to a bigger disaster when dealing with a problem without fully clarifying the situation first.

In August 2015, a gas explosion occurred in Tianjin, China. The firefighters arrived on the scene at the beginning of the explosion without first clarifying that chemical gas and liquid were on the site, so they doused the fire with water. The result backfired and it provided more favorable conditions for subsequent explosions causing more loss of life and property.

When making a purchase in a store, we often get this experience: when we encounter poor service, the clerk may offer coupons or give discounts on the purchase made that day, trying to downplay the event. However, what the customer expects is an actual improvement, not some hush money. Counterproductively, this only makes the situation worse and the customer feels more resentful towards the store, so much so that they usually make up their mind not to come back again at that moment.

Warranty is the Minimum Quality Requirement

There is a very useful quality technique—the ability to control the failure-free time of a product. Why do they want to control it? It is because when buying a product, the customer expects the money they spend can give them confidence and dependence in return, which means they want the product to work and function in the way they expect. This is also a non-contractual expectation of the product. But it is impossible for the product to function forever, so manufacturers need to calculate the period of time a product stays failure-free and take it as an ideal indicator.

Consequently, quality experts launch a series of techniques: when designing, they use parts and components that reach a certain level of quality to make the product and use statistical tools to calculate the mean time between failures (MTBF) of the product. Finally, they use the highly accelerated stress screening (HASS) to rule out non-robust products, so the remaining products have statistically failure-free life. Behind this approach is the cost and profit calculation and there are even business opportunities of follow-up services hidden in it. Before researching and developing a product, companies should consider:

1. Cost, selling price, profit margin;

2. Market distribution and sales volume;

3. Warranty period, full life cycle, and MTBF;

4. Maintenance cycle, repair cycle, update cycle, and support methods;

5. Upgrade and update

Among the five points above, the first two are business considerations, the third and fourth are products and services considerations, and the last one is about future extension development. If you can accurately control the third one, you can accurately calculate the customer's overall cost, service cycle, and the required resources for maintenance and support.

The secret of success in product and service design lies here. The longer the warranty period, the happier the customer, but the less the seller earns. On the contrary, the shorter the MTBF, the unhappier the customer, but the more the seller earns. The answer to how to find a balance between these two is called product strategy which is determined by quality control. Now the importance of quality is clearly shown here.

Chapter 7

Product and Service Suitability

After the product is sold, the challenge for the company is to maintain the normal function and the corresponding operation support and maintenance within the product life cycle. Thus, the suitability of products and services is the most important support for the establishment and maintenance of word-of-mouth.

All companies need to know how to cope with *stress* or *pressure* on their products and services in the market. They should preplan and prepare for it so that they are not in a panic when a problem occurs and invite complaints. For example, the challenges of product quality under different environmental conditions, the cultural differences in the way products are used, the difficulty of logistics, the maintenance of logistics support systems, and a stable source of spare parts. These are difficulties (i.e. stresses) every company encounters in long-term business operations, so they should establish and prepare corresponding *suitability* for each of the *stress* mentioned above.

This comprehensive ability to effectively maintain and cost-effectively repair functional specifications is called product and service suitability which is what this chapter is all about. It is easy to understand this ability, but it is a great challenge to follow it because you have to first deal with two things to maintain this ability:

➤ Factors to consider to effectively *maintain* functional specifications

   ✓ Environmental suitability

   ✓ Suitability of operational conditions

✓ Quality of design

✓ Quality of material

✓ Quality of manufacturing

✓ Quality of packaging, storage, and transportation

➢ Factors to consider to cost-effectively *repair* functional specifications

✓ Proper maintenance of product technology and service specification when they change

✓ Qualified technical and service personnel

✓ Adequate and suitable tools and materials

✓ Quick response

✓ Flexible handling of the situation

✓ Ensure sufficient resources required for support

In addition to all traditional manufacturing methods, the suitability of products and services is about the company's competitive strength in the product life cycle, and since sustainability management greatly relies on the reputation of products and services, once the reputation goes bad, the company faces a crisis of survival. The problem is that the time the suitability last should be as long as the time the product last in the market to maintain positive word of mouth. As a result, companies should take the long view and deepen their efforts, so their road to business success can last for a long time with a sustainable quality of products and services.

In order to maintain the suitability of products and services, there has to be close integration with logistics support. Together they assemble two competitive forces for the company. The greater the product suitability, the lighter the burden of logistics support. Conversely, the heavier the burden of logistics support, the higher the usage cost, and relatively, the higher the customer dissatisfaction. Under this interpretation, you may think that the higher the better for the product suitability in the R&D and manufacturing stages, but this is not the case. You should also take the cost into account—the greater the product suitability, the higher the cost of R&D and manufacturing. In this case, the product lost its relative price competitiveness.

This further brings to another conclusion, that is, you have to balance product suitability both with cost and with logistics support. Certainly, if you take a boutique strategy, you can invest more to improve the suitability as great as possible to have customers speak highly of your product. On the other hand, if you take an affordable popular brand strategy, you do not have to spend too much on the suitability in the early stage and the support in late-stage. Instead, you have to spend more on marketing and advertising because the value of the product in one fashion season only last till the end of the season, so all you have to do is to reach the highest sales, and then you can move on to the next one.

Take sedan as an example, a well-known sedan brand claimed to give a ten-year or 200,000 kilometers warranty. It has invested a lot in research and development to achieve the best reliability, maintainability, and safety, so it could give a warranty longer than most other car brands. Relatively, the price of the car is 30% higher than the average price of other cars in the same class. Assuming that the brand's reputation value is excluded, there are a few things the consumer should consider: does the exceeding price of the car compensate for the ten-year maintenance fee when buying other cars? What are their respective chances of a breakdown? In the event of a breakdown, does the consumer have to endure the transportation inconvenience and pay for additional transportation costs when the car is under repair? How safe is this car in the event of a breakdown or a car accident when compared with other cars? How much does it cost to deal with the aftermath of the accident?

From the example above, it involves the ease of use, safety, logistics support capabilities, and the allocation of costs between buyer and seller. Therefore, before adopting this strategy, automakers must clearly analyze all competitive conditions and consumer expectations and adopt corresponding methods of R&D, manufacturing, marketing, and management within the company.

Save for a Rainy Day

When the United States launched satellites into space in the early years, they used the most primitive 8-bit processors with functionality that was much simpler than any modern personal computer for the controller. Why did they use such a simple thing? It was relatively easy to control satellites, so it did not need to be too complicated. But in order to counter the extreme cold, extreme heat, various cosmic rays, and possible collisions in space, this simple computer was not so simple in terms of suitability. It should pass the most rigorous quality and environmental testing of all time on Earth and the costs of parts and materials, as well as the testing costs, have far exceeded our understanding of the cost of ordinary electronics. This is an example that shows the suitability for environmental conditions.

Thirty years ago, a German Siemens engineer provided technical training for a weapons procurement project. One day, when he walked by the warehouse and saw a pile of vacuum tube devices on the ground, he asked: "why are these communication devices not properly packaged and stored?" "These are scrapped devices," replayed. "What? In Germany, we repair and pack these old devices properly for backup because the future microelectronic devices are unable to withstand nuclear explosions and electromagnetic waves!"

Thirty years later, the United States has developed a powerful electromagnetic rail gun which was installed on the warship with the ability to smash the enemy's high-tech electronic equipment at any time! The reminder of the German engineer comes to mind again. This is an example that shows suitability against military threats.

There is a great connection between suitability and promise keeping (whether it is a profit-making promise to shareholders or a promise to consumers), if there is a problem with suitability, all efforts are for naught no matter how much money spend on advertising or how eloquent the endorser is.

Suitability and Satisfaction

He who wants to stand out among the many competitors should make a product that exceeds in every aspect. However, if the cost is too high, it reduces the price competitiveness, so the important issue is how to make the most competitive product under the most cost-effective conditions. At the same time, the company should also take profit and customer satisfaction into account.

Satisfaction is a lagging indicator because it is the data obtained through market research. So how to make sure you can achieve the goal of satisfaction in advance? Is there a leading indicator for it? Yes, suitability! You can most cost-effectively achieve the highest customer satisfaction as long as you can identify various needs customers have when using products, organize them systematically, and transform them into designing indicators and service processes.

More than a decade ago when Qingdao Haier Special Electric Appliance has just taken off, I remembered their advertisement slogan was, "we will be at your door within 30 minutes after calling for repair, and the repair will be done within one hour." I had doubt about it at that time, but now Haier's home appliances have penetrated the White House and it is one of the world's best brands. This is a very successful case of service suitability.

Sakura Range Hoods, another older brand, has made a refreshing promise of a lifetime oil filter free replacement service. You may ask, "then there is no follow-on business, right?" On the contrary, their customers have children and when they start a new family someday, they will bring the most promising and genuine products with them to their new home as well.

The two brands both guarantee after-sales service, but the customer satisfaction programs are all pre-planned with a carefully calculated cost; a product designed with reliability and maintainability as well as the establishment of a huge support service system, and that is why they dared make such a bold promise to customers.

Let's Pointing Our Fingers at Others

The ultimate goal of all business activities is to achieve business goals, which can be done only when all departments within the company cooperate together to analyze customers' needs and distribute these needs to each department for implementation. But we often notice that most companies focus on two departments—sales and R&D—for they only care about *the ability to bring out a design* and *the ability to sell it out*.

After using advertising and marketing to motivate customers to buy and successfully sell the product, what comes next are expressions of dissatisfaction from consumers. These complaints are the customer's substantive opinions from which you can really understand their needs, but they may not be completely and correctly interpreted and dealt with. Instead of being sent to design and production or even logistics supply, they are trapped between two lines of defense called customer service and quality assurance, so the problem is always left unsolved.

Market needs should go through the process of conversion and be internalized into the performance responsibilities of various departments in the business process. These responsibilities include: complete collection of needs; correct interpretation of needs that is converted into design goals; correct conversion of design results into manufacturing processes; quality monitoring that accurately implements manufacturing processes; finished products that pass rigorous suitability certification; logistics system that coordinates with suitability results; service team with experience in specialty product and support process as well as good customers service skills. In this process, the upstream output should be responsible for the downstream input, which are the internal customers mentioned in Total Quality Management (TQM). These closely linked services should get satisfactory results first so that customers can get perfect products and services in the market.

Get Ahead of the Game

The management theory started by the late Mr. Y. C. Wang, the former head of the Formosa Plastics Group, when he was working in a rice shop was familiar to many people. He won people's hearts by calculating customers' consumption of rice and filling it up for them in advance.

There was this interesting story spread on the Internet: after the sewers made by Germans in Qingdao, Shandong Province at the end of China's Qing Dynasty having been used for nearly a century, people can still find spare parts for maintenance within two meters of the faulty parts of the sewers. How surprising such far-sighted thinking is! If you were them, would you be as considerate to your customers as they were? Companies that embraces traditional business methods would not because they want customers to come back for logistics and backup materials to keep their business running. But what does it look like from the customer's perspective? Are your customers glad to "have to" rely on you forever? If the answer is no, then you should understand that when doing business, it is important to put yourself in customers' shoes, so they can see your efforts and attentiveness. Even if they no longer need to rely on you after buying products, they will not feel hesitate to buy other products from you again. This is the brand identity. As mentioned in *Chapter 2*, the goal of the branded company is to earn the greatest brand equity, not the greatest profit.

For equipment sales in the Western industry, the stages of service development are listed as follows:

1. Providing products for customers to use;
2. Providing products for customers to improve production and satisfy the needs of their customers' customers;
3. Providing new technologies to help customers develop products needed in the future and innovate their business.

Suppliers not only consider their own business performance but also accompany their customers to create a "new game" in a highly competitive market and build a community of shared future with customers to grow together and develop together.

Want to Drive Customers away? Keep Ignoring Them!

Refusing to answer the question and answering explicit question ambiguously are the fastest and most effective way to turn off your customers. When customers ask for an answer, a solution, or a promise but get an empty answer, they can sense your insincerity immediately and are unlikely to visit your business again.

Why do you refuse to answer the question or answer explicit question ambiguously? There is no answer at all! Otherwise, you will answer it. But why there is no answer? A successful business is to make the service recipient gain a fairly satisfactory experience. If you are unable to give solid answers to questions asked by them, your service is defective, imperfect, or inadequately prepared. So behind the given answer, it actually shows how adequately you prepare for the service. Moreover, it is this degree of adequacy that determines your chance of success.

In a more outstanding service, the service provider is not only able to answer questions but is also able to get ahead of the game by preparing and providing answers even before being asked. This further gives a feeling of "you can truly read my mind" for the service recipient, so there is naturally a glow of satisfaction on their faces.

So how do you prepare the so-called *answers*? The answer lies in the needs. The clearer and more correct the needs analysis, the more well-prepared the answer. Of course, it also depends on the owner's ambition and resources used to meet customers' needs. At least, you can—give customers the full right-to-know, make a keen observation with a friendly and considerate attitude, and respond quickly to the customer's request to make up for a deficiency. These are all substantial responses.

One with Courage Makes a Majority

The most basic and effective way to ensure quality is to make every step, every type of materials, and every component as good as possible rather than prepare for redundancy to meet an contingency. The latter only causes confusion and panic in business.

What complexity does it have when adding one more redundancy to the original product? Let's take electromechanical products as an example, it increases:

➢ Spatial and structural design: every entity takes up space, so if the original product is increased in volume, it changes the structure and endurance as well;

➢ Weight and counterweight: the weight is increased when adding an object to the original product. With an increase in weight, there comes the counterweight problem. It shifts the center of gravity and affects the physical stability of the product;

➢ Interface: there have to be more interfaces as well, such as:

＊ Connectors: power connector, signal connector, fluid connector, gas connector, linkage;

＊ Diversions: for spare parts, it should also simultaneously receive real-time information about the operation status of the product and the operating instructions for replacement;

＊ Judgment: under what conditions, the spare part should replace the original part? How to replace it? To what extent is the replacement? How long should the replacement last? All of these questions require a complete judgment process;

＊ Monitoring software and hardware: status monitoring, startup and recovery control of spare parts.

> Maintenance: regular cleaning, maintenance, adjustment, and repair.

As can be seen from these descriptions, it takes additional complexity above just to make up for low-quality parts or systems. As for the question of whether it is worth it or not, it should be measured from both subjective and objective perspectives.

At first glance, it sounds perfectly correct when saying "we should save for a rainy day," but you need to think it through whether it means to prepare the best conditions for the original product and service, or to prepare extra redundancy for them?

Benefit Your Customers is Benefit Yourself

The advantages of making standard parts are mostly beneficial to manufacturers themselves. The reasons are: they are the easiest to produce, manufacturers can buy raw materials in bulk, the production process and the quality inspections and standards are consistent, so they can achieve profit maximization. However, this may not be the same if you take the customer's point of view.

Companies that have used software packages must have a similar experience: there are always some parts of the package that are not suitable for you and need to be modified. This arises from the fact that you want a general purpose tool, but it ends up satisfying no one. It turns out to be "one for all, but fit none."

In an attempt to attract consumers more accurately, customization is all the rage as the market gets more and more competitive. Driven by customization, it is increasingly important to carry out research about market demand and of course, it also increases the complexity when producing products. Furthermore, companies should provide more resources to meet trends of high diversity, low volume production, so the cost is relatively increased as well.

When customers are able to give clear requirements and get a product or service better than they expect, their disappointment is relatively reduced and the brand identity of the company is increased. As for the company, their chances to understand customer satisfaction and to get closer to customers are relatively increased. Customization helps them to develop their competitiveness in a more accurate direction than companies that produce standard products, which are unable to track customer's opinions after selling the products.

Keep a Thing Seven Years and You Will Find a Use for it

Everything has its first time, there are maiden voyage, commencement, opening, live show and so on. When the first time comes, if you are not ready for it, you may end up badly.

Here are some examples of situations where it did not even pass the first barrier. In the opening ceremony of Maokong Gondola in Taipei, Taiwan, there was an unexpected cable car failure occurred and stranded passengers in mid-air for more than 40 minutes. It was the first time the government has built a cable car system and it ended up making such a blunder.

The opening of the Electronic Toll Collection (ETC) system in Taiwan was also a mess that caused huge payment problems for drivers. It also made it difficult for the Ministry of Transportation and Communications, the competent authority, to provide details and explanations to the public. Although the improvement was completed in the end, the reputation has been damaged.

Since the launch of iPhone 7 in 2016 until 2018, there have been problems with it constantly coming up in the market. What's puzzling was that Apple, a company with a dominant position in the global smartphone market, did not come up with an effective solution to solve the problem in the shortest time. Instead, the problem happened again and again, making people wonder if there was something wrong with its internal management.

These three examples are all mechanical and electrical products that have accepted international technical support and passed acceptance testing, but they could not even pass the first barrier of all challenges.

There are complaints from customers and there are numerous problems occur at the moment the product is launched. How to get all the funds and efforts invested in the product back? The pre-shipment inspections and product certifications commonly used in the manufacturing industry cannot guarantee anything. What really matters is the verification of the suitability of products and services.

Simplify the Complicated

It is a common phenomenon that companies tend to follow the footsteps of competitors in an attempt to be more competitive. As a result, they constantly add new features or adopt the latest technology and materials in their products and services. However, this often ends up with an over-designed product or a complicated service that not only increases all sorts of costs like R&D, manufacturing, and testing but also reduces the reliability. They forget the most basic principle: properly meet the needs in the simplest way.

For example, since it required few control functions in the satellite that used an 8-bit motherboard mentioned above, most efforts were put into improving its reliability and maintainability. This adhered to the principle of "properly meet the needs in the simplest way."

The popular environmental protection concept in recent years also makes product design more simplified than before. Excessive parts in product design lead to excessive energy consumption and increase carbon emissions in the manufacturing process as well as the cost of recycling. For this reason, every country establishes rules such as manufacturers are not allowed to exceed their carbon emissions quota when producing products as part of their contributions to saving the earth.

In recent years, another concept of life called Essentialism has been proposed by Greg McKeown. It is about applying the principles of "less but better" to say no to all unnecessary things. In terms of implementation, it is all about choosing carefully to achieve excellence, doing the right thing, and doing it right.

This concept is also applicable to the design of products and services. It is about making the greatest contribution when researching, developing, and manufacturing. By doing the thing that really matters, the decision maker makes the most reasonable judgment on investment for the company.

Does a Good Beginning Really Make a Good Ending?

Even if you know the customer needs your product, you still have to clarify their operation conditions first before selling the product. The biggest shortcoming of product design is to shut yourself up and pay no attention to what's going on around you, assuming the customer's operating environment is the same as the one under standardization.

Many years ago when European cars were just allowed to import to Taiwan, there were consistent complaints about the air conditioning was not strong enough, especially in summer with unbearable sweltering heat. After a series of customer complaints, they finally realized there are basic differences between Taiwan's and Europe's climate in terms of latitude and humidity. In later designs, they especially singled out Taiwan's climate characteristics and improved them accordingly.

In the early stage when the US troops involved in the Gulf War, there were constant reports about failures of weapons and military products on the battlefield. After the maintenance department disassembled and analyzed them, they found there were tiny dust inside these weapons that worn down or stuck them, making them unable to be used. Since they did not encounter these problems often in regular situations, this environmental factor was ignored in design. Fortunately, to them, there was no decisive battle at that time, so there was still time to make improvements.

There are all sorts of strange reasons that affect the normal use of the product. Besides dust, there are animal hair, insects, high heat and high humidity, local power supply, operation conditions and habits, and signal loading and signal carrying capacity that service technicians should remind the design department to pay special attention to. Even if there are things they do not anticipate in advance, they should collect and analyze special environmental conditions of the consumer market from failure cases and return the results to the design department to start the design improvement process.

What's more important is that designers should always keep various operational challenges and environmental stresses in mind!

Chapter 8

Logistics Support

Logistics is often misunderstood and underestimated. We often see it as the process of packaging, inventory, and transportation and ignore the original roots and definitions of logistics—military science that deals with the procurement, maintenance, and transportation of military supplies, facilities, and personnel. It is a behavior that precisely calculates and plans for a specific operation, which means the supply support for all resources required from the beginning of the operation (market sales volume) to the service supports (deployment numbers of service) during the full product life cycle.

Another compound noun is logistics support, which is the operating system that provides the results of all the efforts mentioned in previous chapters to the market and defines the content (including the work items of maintenance and repair) in accordance with distribution areas and expiration date of products and services. Without logistics support, all efforts in design, production, and marketing are in vain, especially for companies that have expanded their business internationally. Once there are problems with their products abroad, a lack of logistics support can cause the entire service to be chaotic and ineffective.

There are two types of logistics support. The one that supports daily operations is called operations support, such as warehousing, packaging, logistics and transportation, materials handling, replenishment of consumables, management tools and resources, etc. The other type of logistics is the resource requirements derived from poor quality, customer complaints and so on, including backup materials, maintenance tools, testing instruments or methods, analysis and preparation, the development and update of the technical manual, and the training and certification of maintenance personnel—these are called maintenance support. Generally, logistics support is an overall logistics maintenance program and the establishment and deployment of the logistics team, energy, and resources.

The daily operations support part mainly focuses on maintaining the functionality and suitability of products and services at the level that meets customers' needs so that companies can be more competitive in the market.

The maintenance part mainly focuses on repairing products and services to quickly and cost-effectively make them continue to function as the customer expects after the failure occurs.

These two types of logistics support—one for maintaining and the other for repairing—function cooperatively with each other that allow products and services to be constantly maintained at the same level and in the same direction of the brand.

What's interesting is product and service suitability and logistics support are two elements that can and should interact with each other in brand performance. If you provide products and services with strong suitability, it reduces the needs for logistics support and strengthens the brand identity accordingly. On the other hand, if the suitability is weak, the needs as well as the costs for logistics support are increased together with the chances of weakening your brand identity.

Strong suitability means good products and services but higher upfront investment cost to achieve suitability goals, so it weakens the price competitiveness.

On the other hand, if the suitability is weak, the price competitiveness is relatively strong, so it is easier to sell them, but what comes next are higher failure rate and lower service quality. This is bad news for both suppliers and consumers because it means a higher final cost, which is usually not easy to be predicted and controlled. The cost can be maintenance costs, operating costs, disaster costs, medical costs, loss of life and property, and even social cost, not to mention the possibility of losing the brand image and development opportunities, which are the real disasters for the company.

Therefore, from the perspective of building a brand, the optimal allocation and application between the cost of suitability and logistics support play a significant role in gaining brand awareness and brand identity in the market. The key of successful customer experience lies here. The balance between the allocation and application of these two depends on different customer types' expectations for products and services and the company's brand positioning and orientation.

The following figure clearly shows this corresponding relation:

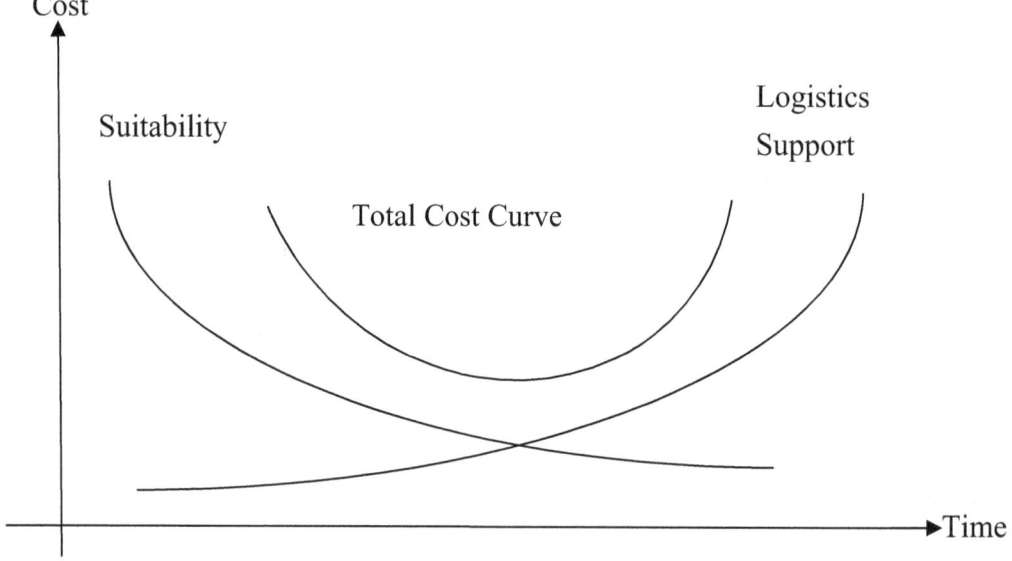

Gain Decisive Victory a Thousand Miles away

Employees responsible for logistics are innocent. For one thing, they do not know what R&D and manufacturing are doing; for another, they do not know what is going on in the market. The only thing they know is when the front line customer service is turned upside down by customers, they have to serve as firefighters and rush to rescue.

There is a general perception that logistics is responsible for supporting the market. Everything that happens in the market affects customer satisfaction, so if there is a lack of supply, the service strength declines or even disappears. The logistics department is obliged to provide the information about product consumption, quality problems, and suitability problems to the R&D and manufacturing departments so as to take improvement actions to eliminate the root cause of failure and maximize product benefits in the market.

"Business is like a battlefield" is a famous saying in business, which not only refers to all efforts you make to be the first to market or price war but, in fact, it also refers to the core strength of the brand, which sees logistics analysis as the brain; requirement development, innovation and R&D, product suitability, and market service as the arms. This is the model that match military logistics operations and can lead you to a successful business in whatever field you choose.

Instead of getting close to the market and taking market needs as their development goals, if the owner still cannot get rid of the manufacturer's thinking and habits, sees product functionality as its development orientation, and considers themselves to be a contract manufacturer, then the company always falls far behind international brands. Their chances to build a brand successfully seem to be no end in sight if the role of logistics is still undervalued without changing it completely.

Layout and Resources Support

Before a car dealer enters a new market, they have to first consider the size of the auto repair shop, the number of service areas, the maintenance equipment, the types and quantities of parts, the inspection and repair time of various damages, then the number of maintenance technicians, and finally, the average turn-around time (number of vehicles per day). Even if they can sell the car without thinking about these questions, the poor maintenance quality still stops them from getting higher performance. Now with this example, it is obvious that the market is closely related to logistics and services.

After the Fukushima Daiichi nuclear disaster, flights to Fukushima suddenly were filled with high-level purchasing directors from global branded companies. There were many semiconductor component manufacturers in Fukushima Prefecture that supplied many of the world's largest technology factories. With the tsunami and nuclear disaster, many assembly lines have been affected that severely reduced the production capacity. International buyers arrived Fukushima right after the accident for fear that it would soon run out of stock and affect the mass production of end products, so they tried to get the firsthand information about the disaster's impact on the supply chain.

When logistics resources are controlled by others, companies may face a cruel situation. The logistics maintenance of large-scale systems involves some particularly important parts, which are not so commonly used in normal maintenance, but once the equipment gets old, it is highly possible that they may get an out-of-stock response. There are two ways to solve it, one is to buy the latest version of the same product which can cost them an arm and a leg.

The other option is called cannibalization, which is to gather all the failed parts into a subsystem and banish it, but this almost abandons the entire subsystem, so it is the last resort. An inferior method is to repair or produce these failed parts without acquiring original manufacturing technology transfer, but by doing so, they are equivalent to inferior products. When these inferior products are assembled back into the subsystem, the quality and suitability of the entire system begin to decrease. What's worse is if they are used between subsystems to operate the system, then these quality defects are spread throughout the whole system, and finally reduces the system-wide task execution capabilities. Logistics is not just as simple and unprofessional as passing from one hand to the other; on the contrary, it is an important factor that affects the success or failure of the task.

Put Yourself in the Client's Shoes

Cost and profit (or benefit) are the biggest concerns for both buyers and sellers, whether it refers to transactions in business-to-business (B to B) or business-to-customer (B to C).

There are two types of costs in the life cycle of products and services. Before the moment they are put into the buyer's hands, there are costs of R&D, production, advertising, logistics, services, and overhead, which are all counted as the supplier's cost of sales and it is relatively fixed. The price of the product or service should be higher than all these costs. The exceeding part is the profit, otherwise there is no commercial value in this transaction at all.

The other type of costs is called cost of ownership, such as procurement, operations (manpower, utility charges and so on), maintenance, repair, and disposal, which should be paid by the buyer. This cost is a variable cost that changes in relation to variations in products and services. So what are these variations?

1. Poor quality of the product, including inadequate suitability. If there are consistent failures, it affects the customer's benefits and other derived costs. Additionally, the maintenance costs outside the warranty period should be paid by the buyer.

2. Missing, delays, and poor quality of spare parts affects customer's benefits and other derived costs.

3. Operations and maintenance-related problems: when the manual is inaccurate and the personnel is not well trained, it leads to failures caused by operational malfunctions during operations and maintenance of the product and affects customer's benefits and other derived costs. If the responsibility is vague and unclear, the buyer should also take the loss.

4. The cost of workplace accidents from any possible accidents caused by products, including loss and insurance costs.

From the cost structure mentioned above, it clearly shows that the buyer's cost of ownership may occur anytime during the product life cycle. It increases unexpected expenditures and threatens financial stability if a clear way to prevent it is unavailable. From this, we can further draw a conclusion that if there are problems like poor quality, inadequate suitability, poor logistics support, and insufficient operations and maintenance technology transfer, it increases the buyer's cost of ownership and eventually makes them stay away from these products.

Do not Make the Problem Worse

After selling products, logistics undertakes the basic support needs and problems that come from quality, product suitability, and service suitability. In these support problems, the severity may be high or low, the distance may be near or far, the situation may be urgent or trivial, and the amount of support required may be large or small, so it is relatively difficult to control these problems in advance. And again, it also involves the evaluation of customer satisfaction and market reputation.

It should start to simulate from the operational task scenarios, including the changes in various types of environmental stress. For example, in the market with the highest temperature, what may happen when you play videos on loop with a mobile phone? Would it cause the battery overheat or software anomalies? Or, under the situation when the vent hole of a machine is blocked, what component failure does it cause first? When the transformer of a working machine fails or is unstable, what components fail the most?

The reason for starting to simulate from the operational task scenarios and the changes of various types of environmental stress is that the place where product failure occurs is the real-life situation the logistics department has to deal with in reality. If it is an enterprise customer, the logistics department should send appropriate testing equipment, spare parts, maintenance tools, and qualified maintenance personnel to the customer. If it is an individual consumer, after collecting the failure phenomenon at the repair station, it should also prepare maintenance tools mentioned above and deliver it in time.

The logistics department of a competitive company has to put more efforts than that of a traditional company and they often make these efforts:

1. Analyze the background of the failure, such as season, operation timing and duration, operation method and load, and the surface phenomenon of the failure.
2. The time they takes to be on the scene, failure detection and analysis, repair time, and types and quantity of spare parts they have used.
3. Failure position and associated failures. The first three steps are called data collection.
4. The next one is data analysis. Take markets, customer attributes, and seasons that are categorized according to failure types and definition to carry out the analysis of reliability, maintainability, and availability of the product.
5. Find out the root cause of failure, assign the responsibility, and ask the department responsible to propose a thorough improvement strategy. The most important part of this step is to compare with the failure mode and effects analysis (FMEA) conducted at the beginning of the design and to implement or correct the design content according to the cause of failure.
6. Continue to monitor whether the product failure is improved, compare the improvement effect, and repeat step 1.to step 5.

Easy to Love but Hard to Raise

When observing challenges from the perspective of logistics and transportation, we can see many common challenges many companies share in this aspect:

1. Unstable price of raw materials makes it difficult to set price. Once the market is used to the price it accepts, it is difficult to change it because it causes an anchoring effect on consumers' willingness to pay.

2. Unstable quality of raw materials leads to reputational risk. A while ago, Mitdub, a soy sauce company in southern Taiwan, added Jin Lan soy sauce, another soy sauce brand in Taiwan, into its products due to a lack of sources of imported beans. It caught the market by surprise but they were inexcusable, not to mention the spread of fake cooking oil from upstream to downstream has left many food manufacturers to be wrongfully accused.

3. The transportation cost changes with the oil price that makes the profit margin uncontrollable, and when the estimation of transportation cost slightly goes wrong, the company suffers a financial loss.

4. Packaging and preservation: when the company is careless about the quality of packaging materials, methods or preservation environment, the damage caused is not merely a matter of money but of degraded quality and customer safety. The loss incurred is like paying double for nothing.

5. Risks in transportation: such as storms, erosion, and looting in maritime transport; turbulence in air transport; vibrations, theft, and pollution in land transport, are all risks of loss.

The logistics department faces these risks in every batch of product every single day. They are the keys to the success or failure of delivery and they are not just problems in R&D and manufacturing process but problems in delivery process—they are of no less importance than producing a product!

Chapter 9

Market Service

In all business activities, service is the most interactive and "closest " one to the customer. If it is a successful service, on the bright side, it increases sales performance; on the dark side, it at least decreases the degree of dissatisfaction. But if the service fails, all previous efforts are in vain. In other words, service providers are the key players who give the last push to deal with the various needs of customers. The following roles and functions are the connotation of service:

- Attacker—he who increases performance

- Defender—he who reduces customer churn

- Corporate endorser—he who increases the reputation of a company

- Brand ambassador—he who improves corporate image

As a result, branded companies should not use traditional thinking that regards employees in customer service as mediocre workers; instead, they should re-recognize the importance of service, pay more attention to these employees, and give them better training and treatment to create a sense of unity with all employees. In this way, they naturally treat customers with respect and offer good service to them, presenting a new image and new style of the company' service.

Service is to help others have their work done or to solve problems for others. Service providers who show a gesture of respect and modesty are humble. The definition of service in *ISO—The Service Industry Quality Management(1992)* is: "A *service* is an intangible output and is the result of a process that includes at least one activity that is carried out at the interface between the supplier (provider) and the customer."

To sum up, service is to use labor or tangible products to work and solve problems for others in a humble manner and, at the same time, it should meet the needs of the service recipient.

It is important for the service provider to know the type of the customer they serve to give the right product and service they want based on different demand characteristics. Generally, there are two types of customers, enterprise customer and individual customer, and based on the characteristics of each type, there are many classification methods:

The types of enterprise customers:

- Government and public enterprise
- Private listed company
- Small and medium enterprise (SME)
- School
- Hospital
- Non-profit organization, foundation, juridical association
- Privatization of public-owned enterprise
- Government outsourcing companies
- Upstream supplier

This type of customers should comply with specific procedures for buying and selling established by government or enterprise itself. The specification and course of performance are necessary conditions for providing service to them with the 4R (right law, right time, right quality, and right place) as the way to honor the agreement. Internationally, enterprise customer service has developed in the following stages:

- Sell products to customers;

- Sell products to assist customers in promoting their internal business processes;

- Remind customers of new trends in the market and new upgrading technologies;

- Act as a partner with customers and enable them to expand their business.

From this advanced point of view, if the company still remain at the product selling level when providing business-to-business service, it will end up playing an insignificant role in business.

Analysis according to characteristics of individual customer:

- Career

- Gender

- Age

- Professional background

- Cultural background

- Socioeconomic status

- Lifestyle

- Consumption orientation

These analysis above are just the broadest categories. The variability alone is high enough when companies with different types of products and services encounter different people. If taking factors like season, trend, purpose, urgency, and personality traits into account, there is going to be a variety of ways to serve. When a service provider is handling customer needs, they should pay a special attention to observe the type of the customer, develop a systematic service system with an agile mind, and offer support to the customer during the service lifecycle, so that the service is not inadequate that increases customer churn or the loss of the company. This is the time when the service provider can best show their individual service characteristics, which is also emphasized in the previous paragraphs that branded companies must think creatively and reshape their service skills and service styles.

Classified by service stages:

- Pre-sales service

- Sales service

- After sales service

Pre-sales focuses on the development, guidance and confirmation of needs; sales focuses on delivery and acceptance, usage and maintenance instructions, and training; after sales focuses on maintenance and repair. It is important to allow customers to complete their purchase satisfactorily from beginning to end even without a detailed and rigorous contract.

In general, it is all about giving customers a grateful and unforgettable experience—this is the highest level of service!

Sincerity and Humor are the Best Qualities

Standing on the front line, service providers have to interact with people—both within and outside the company—who have different characters and personalities and they also have to manage to turn dissatisfaction into satisfaction within the shortest time.

Internally, service providers should make a comparative analysis of the advantages of their own products and that of other competitors, which alone requires them to be familiar with both their own and others' products. They need to have strong confidence in quality first before they can give a firm promise to the customer. This is more than training—this is established by long-term product performance, which has something to do with whether or not the service provider is proud of their company's product quality.

The more confidence they have in their own products, the more convincing they are to customers. So whether the front-line customer service representatives can face customers with full confidence all depends on whether the company can cooperate together to make good products. If the quality is not good enough, the suitability is not adequate enough, the logistics supply is not fast enough, and the service process is not reasonable enough, even with the most powerful and peerless skills, it is still impossible for them to make a brick without a straw.

Externally, there are various difficulties when facing different customers with different habits and attitudes, especially in an aging society. There are more and more elderly consumers who need to be treated with more patience to interact and communicate with them because of their decline in physical health. Additionally, there are hostile customers who give destructive criticism that is unimaginable for ordinary people and sometimes they may even use violence. At this time, customer service representatives must show a higher degree of emotional intelligence to tolerate them and properly calm them down.

How to properly calming down dissatisfied customers? Sincerity first! If it is your fault, then you have to admit it honestly. Stop beating around the bush, promise to improve within the shortest time, and actually do what you say. If it is not your fault, then explain it patiently based on facts and senses. Of course, the so-called unreasonable and hostile customers do not buy it and ignore this reasonable procedure. At this time, you might as well be humorous and treat it as a joke by saying "smile, you're on camera!"

Humor is a trait a person were born with that is difficult to acquire. A person with a sense of humor can be both active and calm; they can separate their own emotions from those of their clients, analyze the problem, and get to the points quickly; they are even calm in the middle of a storm and can turn a serious situation into a humorous one. Good service providers choose to work in the service industry for a reason, not because they have nothing else to do.

A Good Beginning is Half the Battle

Everyone's expression of opinions varies with personality, especially when they have different career and needs. On top of that, if people do not fully understand their own needs, it greatly affects how well they can express them. So the first step of service is to clarify the needs of the person. If you make a mistake in this very step, then all the efforts you make later are going to be totally wasted. This is why communication is the first step of service, and it is not an exaggeration to say that it is also the most important step for the company for it determines the success or failure of the business.

Usually, when it comes to listening, it means to clearly understand the customer's needs, but when the customer is unable to express them clearly, the service provider needs to patiently guide them and ask the details of what they want. Do not randomly accept orders just for higher sales performance; otherwise, there may be endless troubles following you in the future.

For many contract manufacturers, one of their habits is to produce products according to the contract specifications. It is generally believed that these products only need to go through the quality control process required by the consignor, but when so many problems come later, they do not even realize that the main cause of these problems is that they did not clarify the needs in the first place. I was once talking to a contract manufacturer and I asked: "do all of you understand the environmental requirements of these parts you produce?" "We have manufactured them according to specifications provided by the consignor, including environmental stress screening, and these parts we produce are assembled inside the finished products, so there is no way they are exposed to the external environment," he answered. "How about the internal environment? Isn't the temperature within the enclosed space higher than the temperature outside? Isn't the electromagnetic interference generated more directly within the internal circuit?" I asked. "They have to take care of it on their own, we just follow the specifications they provide." Finally, I asked, "then in the event of product failure, does it ultimately refer to the failed part or the 'product' as a whole? Which one will they blame, themselves, or you guys who are responsible for providing these parts?" He was rendered speechless.

In many public construction projects, the client is usually the user or the project manager, so they do not really know the details of the technical conditions so well as the system vendor. Moreover, even when users have slightly different requirements for operational features, it can subtlety change the design of the system. If you do not clarify the requirements, there will be great disputes as to the performance of contract duties in the future, a delay in the project, and a huge loss of on both sides.

The requirements in the service industry focus on purpose, timeliness, privacy, comfort, and safety. Among these requirements, privacy is particularly important that involves safety and affects individual, business, military, and national security. Nowadays, with the developed and prosperous online media, it has a even greater impact than before, so the details of communication and implementation are fairly important as well.

In minor cases, there are situations like getting the date of the wedding wrong, getting the product transportation and storage conditions wrong, getting the product testing and certification regulations wrong and so on. There are countless cases of making mistakes in the first step (i.e. communication) that result in endless financial and security problems. The correctness of communication is really the top priority for all transactions!

Best Way to Escape from Your Problems is to Solve Them

Requirements come in different forms in different industries. In engineering, they are clearly listed, such as operating methods, operation mode, functional specification, warranty, maintenance, and logistics support. The requirements for consumer products are relatively simple, mostly functional requirements. As for the service industry, they are mainly about things like purpose as mentioned in the previous section. The habits of customers in the same industry are basically consistent, but they also vary with the complexity of the product and their own experience.

Take the walkie-talkie as an example. If it is used in a work team, the purchaser should require signal strength, communication distance, waterproof capability, moisture resistance, number of channels, central control and so on. If the service provider can guide the purchaser to express these requirements clearly and get a deeper understanding and confirmation of the procurement specifications, the purchaser is definitely more satisfied with the service.

In the personal service industry, although we can get rich enough services to fulfill our own desires with various applications (apps) and online platforms for any kinds of entertainment and make the fastest purchase with them, the service itself can go further and better. ZAPPOS, the custom-made shoe service founded by Chinese American Tony Hsieh, could provide wedding shoes in one night for the customer who lived several states away. Besides the service of fresh meat delivery, the meat shop, Frank, also provided customers with immediate cooking and consumption service. Both of them offer services that directly fulfill and satisfy customers' personal needs rather than try to make customers open their wallets.

Many designers and planners have a habit of choosing the best solution from their own perspectives. They often communicate with customers from a mindset of persuading rather than of understanding and realizing thoughts of their customers. Over time, they become bench warmers who can only watch others play in the international market.

It Takes Real Efforts to Pull the Chestnuts Out of the Fire for Others

Many people have this common experience: you are busy at work and suddenly you receive a phone call from a sales representative who tries to promote their products. Most of the time, these sales representatives get a resounding "no! I do not have time for this."

When hearing such an answer, the biggest challenge for them is how to control their temper, avoid customer's sharp words and provocations, and make them take out their wallet to buy these products.

This requires a high level of emotional intelligence. As a service provider, you are only a representative of the company, so you do not have to take customer complaints personally and see the malicious words as attacks on you. At the same time, you need to collect the customer's main request as you remove those emotion words from their complaints and give them to the company for improvement. It is also important for you to track the improvement and ask the company to remake the service or product after improvement.

There are two kinds of challenging situations for customer service representatives to handle and they should be included in the SOP. The first one is to deal with customers in bad moods or nitpicking customers during the sales process; the second one is to deal with customers who are very dissatisfied with the products and services after sales, especially verbally abusive customers.

As a result, emotional control and management should be included in the training of service personnel and company have to provide care and emotional release for them whenever they need it during the service process. There was a short story about a counter staff with a particularly good sales performance who was invited to share her experience with other colleagues in the all-hands meeting. She said: "I have hard-of-hearing, so I do not know exactly what customers are complaining about." This is a joke of course, but it shows how important emotional intelligence is for service providers.

There is also a third situation that is not about customer abuse, but a hunger-and-cold-tempt-men-to-steal situation which involves crimes committed by people in socially vulnerable situations. When dealing with this situation, the company has to define the processing method according to its values in advance. In 2014, the owner of a noodle stand in Taiwan found that one of his gas barrels was stolen. Instead of calling the police, he put a note on his stand saying: "please return the gas barrel after it is empty." Sure enough, the reason for stealing the barrel matched this hunger and cold situation—the thief was unable to support his family. Later, he surrendered himself to the police together with the gas barrel. In the end, the police tempered justice with mercy and donated merchandise and money to the family, making this case a touching social service story. Only when a service is filled with warmth can it be deeply rooted in people's hearts.

Shrewd as Snakes

With a diverse customer base, the needs could be large or small, urgent or trivial; financial policies and payment conditions also vary from one to another. In this case, when contacting customers, the service provider needs keen judgment and think fast on their feet all the time.

The training for customer service should also include an understanding of the customer and their background and the level of customer satisfaction. This is sensitivity training for customer service agents. In addition to this, it also requires an eloquence training and a service attitude that shows respect for customers.

One night about thirty years ago, I saw a pre-sale center near my house selling real estate when I went out for a walk with family after dinner, so we walked in. There were so many customers on the site but salespeople were more attentive to well-dressed customers. I was dressing casually with slippers, so not a single salesperson paid attention to me. After standing for a while without getting any attention, I deliberately said to my wife: "how many Cathay Life Insurance shares do we own?" Cathay Life Insurance was the highest priced stock at that time in Taiwan. After hearing what I said, there were several salespeople rashly coming toward us at the same time.

In the era of e-commerce, most services are no longer face-to-face service, so service providers do not judge people by appearance, wealth or background anymore, but they start to judge people by consumption habits and credit history. They do not go after customers who make a one-time large purchase anymore because the instability poses certain risks for financial planning; instead, they choose to go after people who make periodic small purchases.

There is an interesting natural phenomenon that coincides with this theory—as the largest animal on earth, whales grow to such large sizes by eating plankton in the oceans. There are new evaluation methods for e-commerce, such as credit limit, ability to repay, and credit history; there is also a spending limit on the amount of money you have in the e-wallet even in a small purchase, making it simpler and safer.

Who Really Understands You?

Service providers are people like everyone else and they also have feelings. They have family, friends, and other interpersonal relationships to deal with, but when they are at work, they have to abandon their emotions and devote themselves to work. Meanwhile, they also need to put aside their emotions at work to concentrate on customers and give good service to them.

Besides personal incidents, service providers are most affected by the supervisor's attitude in the workplace. If the workload is divided fairly and the workplace dispute is resolved equitably by the supervisor, employees can get along with each other peacefully. Generally speaking, they can keep a healthy state of mind and offer service to customers more calmly and friendly as long as everyone on the team accept their share of the collective workload.

After the company has applied principles of interpersonal communication mentioned above, what's left is to make employees concentrate on their work. In Japan, employees like to do aerobic exercise or morning workout before work, which is quite effective for them to concentrate more on work. However, there is no such practice in European and American companies, but their day always starts with some particularly warm greetings to their colleagues that also has a similar effect.

Either way, if the company can find a way to get employees to focus on work at the beginning of each task, it improves their work efficiency throughout the day.

The Product Can Speak for Itself!

It is *not* completely risk-free for maintenance. Proper maintenance can keep the product functioning normally, but incorrect maintenance can be counterproductive and shorten the life of the product. For example, misdiagnosis leads to erroneous updates, improper use of oil can damage the machine, careless adjustment can reduce precision, improper assembly of consumables can cause malfunctions and so on. All in all, maintenance is also an external intervention for a normally functioning product, so there are also risks.

But what is going to discuss here is another attitude: "all goods sold are non-exchangeable and non-refundable," which, in ancient times means: "Dear guest, you had better think twice before paying, if you want to nitpick after you pay, it is your choice, but we will not take any responsibility." The main purpose behind this is to evade responsibility.

Naturally, the boundaries of rights and obligations in modern transactions are greatly different from those of ancient times. Sellers are not allowed to be so irresponsible after selling products. Almost all civilized countries have fair trade laws and consumer protection laws that explicitly protect consumers' rights and interests, thereby any evasion of responsibility on the part of the seller is not allowed.

Once the quality is reduced, no matter who should pay the cost, customer satisfaction is reduced as well—at least the customer's expectation of the product is reduced that brings complaints about its cost-effectiveness. The market reputation is therefore ruined, and as time goes by, the revenue of the company declines, so in the end, it seems the company will have to lie on the bed they made. If the company would rather let the burden of management responsibility fall fully on the after-sales service, then it is catching at the shadow and losing the substance. It is nothing more than burying their heads in the sand.

It is best to have after-sales service ready just in case and strive to make the product quality better for it is always not a good thing when customer service is needed after sales. It may either damage the business reputation or the seller has to pay back the profit to the customer as compensation. The problem is not whether customer service agents are doing a good job, but whether the upstream produces good products and whether there are good planning and preparation for the entire after-sales service system.

It is a One-off Game

There are some unique products that cannot be stopped once they are turned on, otherwise, it causes interruption to the task, major disasters, or huge losses. For example, the furnace for steelmaking, space vehicles and equipment, military weapons, aircraft, production equipment for semiconductor and electronics, chemical engineering equipment, and precision machine tools. These products have high quality requirements with a very low failure rate and a reduced minimum requirement for after-sales service (or even do not need maintenance at all, but are designed for self-healing or to provide active backup). Some of them are used in special environments that users have to carry out maintenance themselves; as a result, the manufacturer or the seller strives to achieve a very high level of quality in these products.

It is understandable that the cost of launching equipment into space is extremely high. If whenever there is a failure that requires repair, they have to send maintenance personnel and the inspection and maintenance equipment up there again, then the cost is certainly too high for us to imagine. Should the military weapons fail or even inadvertently explode in the event of an enemy attack on the battlefield that leads to the defeat, it involves not only the cost but also the success or failure of the war, then the consequences cannot be measured in terms of money.

Maintenance is like maintaining healthy skin. When the skin is dry, you can moisturize it with skin cream; when it is aging, you can apply exfoliating scrub to it. But if the skin is not well taken care of or you do not drink plenty of water and relax, it continues drying, aging, and getting wrinkles. So do systems and products. If the product already comes with poor pre-shipment quality, when there are new risks incurred from maintenance, the product quality deteriorates quickly. So the company that wants to improve customer satisfaction or even gain more profit through maintenance is not going to get its way easily in this regard.

Products that do not require maintenance are often accompanied by the industry's unique quality conditions, suitability conditions, and system safety regulations which are also very important conditions for competition in the international market. If product manufacturers can develop in this direction, they have the opportunity to make their way to the international market with their own brands.

The procurement issued by the US Department of Energy (DOE) in recent years was even outside the system specifications limits that directly provided space for power generation equipment and specified the amount of electricity to be purchased. The challenge is that energy suppliers should be responsible for power generation efficiency and maintenance costs themselves, which directly tests their comprehensive strength.

Is it Better to Change Customers?

According to business research, the cost of developing a new customer is about 4 to 10 times that of maintaining a regular customer. For every 5% increase in customer retention rate, the profit can be increased by 25% to 125%. All kinds of data emphasize how important it is to keep regular customers.

There has been gradually developed a new term in business administration called "Customer Relationship Management (CRM)" about twenty years ago. It is nothing special than collecting customer data; using statistical analysis to find out important customer bases, characteristics of their company, and their contribution value; understanding the real needs of customers; providing timely assistance for customers' urgent needs, one-on-one interaction, real-time marketing and so on.

This theory is still aimed at improving customer satisfaction but with more practical and scientific methods. It also uses the principle of maximum return on investment and the 80/20 rule to find the top 20 customers who have contributed 80% of total sales of the company to maintain and enhance the relationship with them. These customers are known as key accounts and the management of these customers is called Key Account Management (KAM). I jokingly call it Kiss Ass Management for the fact that most of these managers eventually end up accompanying customers to get up early in the morning to play golf, or accompanying them to dinner parties and paying for other "entertainment" during the day, turning themselves into social-butterfly managers.

Whether it is CRM or KAM, eventually they have to go back to the original point: good products and services (here it refers to logistics services). Since they are regular customers, they have already made their purchase from the company, what's left is their opinions about the purchase. Things that greatly gain satisfaction and positive evaluation include essential technology, excellent products, after-sales maintenance services, logistics support, the stability of customer costs, and the reminder and participation of business direction. Customers with a correct business philosophy should be glad to embrace this overall service rather than accept service that merely caters to their private and personal needs.

Chapter 10

System Integration

So far we have already talked about seven competencies, namely, requirement development, innovation and R&D, system safety, quality management, logistics support, product and service suitability, and customer service. It is time to talk about the one that integrates them all together—*system integration.*

Since it is called integration, it is not like playing a jigsaw puzzle that recruits all the people in charge in every sector to let them express their own opinions and let them go back to do it on their own. Unfortunately, this is a normal situation in most public and private companies. If there is no related interaction between various departments' performance in your company, then they must do it on their own. The same thing happens even on the world's popular Balanced Scorecard (BSC) that every department establishes their performance goals based on the company's business policies. It seems that they all directly make a contribution to the company's business goals, including the level of achievements in business policies, financial goals, and human resources. But things are different when it comes to the working relationships between departments, for example, when the output of department A is the input of department B, should we consider including the satisfaction of department B to department A as one of the important indicators for measuring the performance of department A?

The BSC has been used in the market for a long time and it uses four dimensions—financial dimension, customer dimension, internal process dimension, and learning and growth dimension—to achieve company's vision and strategy. However, after formulating the vision and goals, the company often send the balanced scorecard to every department to develop their respective department goals based on it. It seems logically correct, but the problem is the relevance of internal processes is not closely combined, that is to say, the role of observation and monitoring is not available in the horizontal relationship related to connection and balance between departments. This brings a problem—even if all departments seem to achieve their respective goals, since there is no corresponding and comprehensive evaluation between departments, it is impossible to give balance and control. As a result, many resources are used in double work that different departments work on the same thing and produce the same result. This relationship is shown in the following figure:

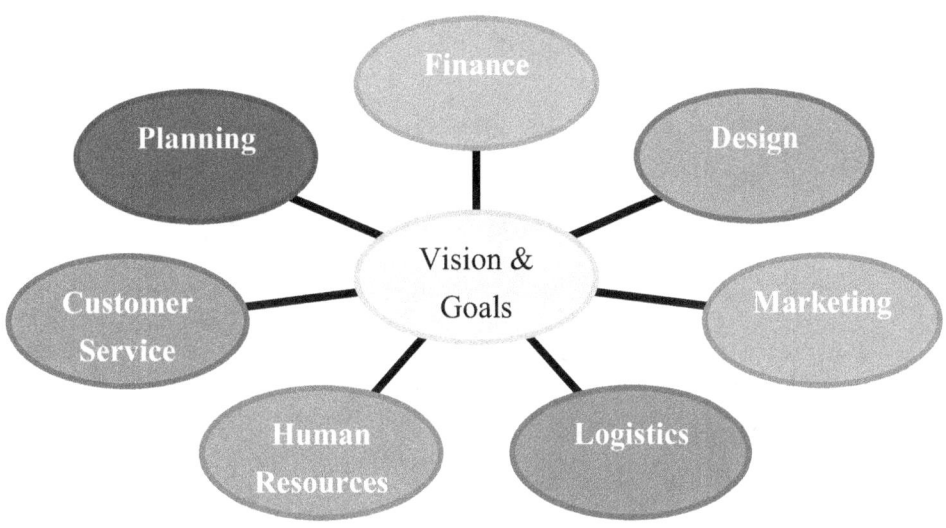

System integration gives solutions to this problem. It takes the pursuit of becoming a branded company as its vision and establishes and connects the nine brand competencies proposed in this book as strategies. Starting from *Requirement Development*, which identifies the specific content that supports products and services; to *Innovation and R&D*, which converts needs into specifications; to *System Safety*, which ensures risks associated with specifications are completely eliminated and products are safe to use; to *Quality Management*, which controls the quality of products and services to ensure they meet or exceed specifications; to *Product and Service Suitability*, which guarantees maximum benefits and cost-effectiveness for customers; to *Logistics Support*, which provides all resources customers need; to *Customer Service*, which delivers the results of all the previous efforts to customers. *System Integration* then connects and balances the previous seven steps to produce the greatest satisfaction with the least resources.

This concept is shown as follows:

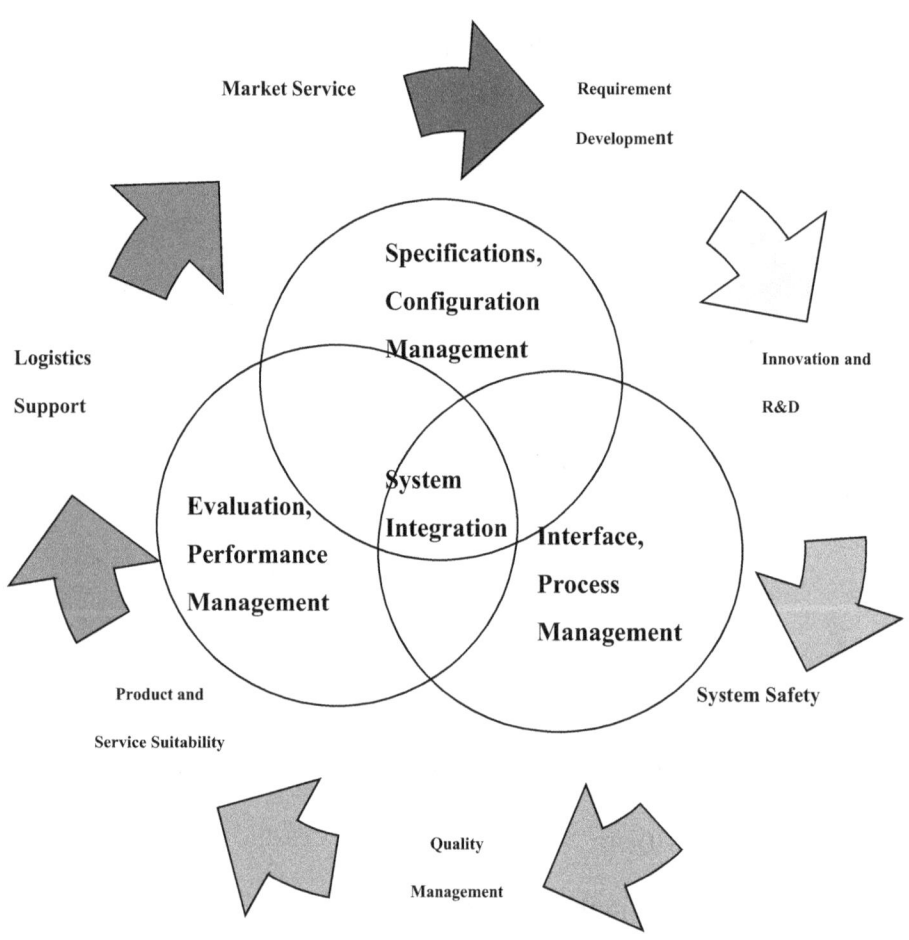

There is a sequential correlation among these eight brand competencies which forms a complete and endless sustainable cycle. The sequence of these processes is arranged in order of occurrence and the output of each process should meet the input requirements of the next process.

The Puzzle is Not Complete With a Missing Piece

Theoretically, the division of labor is the most cost-effective mode of production, but it also creates a serious problem that each department only focuses on its own duty. The power and responsibility that come with the division of labor make departments even more daunting to exceed the prescribed limit, so much so that every department does not know and does not care what other departments are doing. These two practices are the reasons why people become very conservative in the workplace.

But is this wrong? No, what is wrong is there is no integration to bring the performance of every department together and make them serve other departments in the same way as they serve customers.

The design and R&D department believes no design no product and the secret to success lies in design. The manufacturing department believes without manufacturing, the design is just empty talk. The quality assurance department believes that without quality control, the customer is not satisfied with the manufactured products at all. The logistics department believes without logistics, even the best product is merely sales figures and the customer's willingness to come back again is limited. The service department also believes without service, there is a lack of human touch to serve as a bridge between product and customer and lose the opportunity to handle customer complaints.

These perspectives above are correct, but the problem lies in the fact that every department does not know how to cooperate with each other. There is a lack of professional understanding, a lack of understanding of other's position, a lack of process integration, and a lack of connection between performance indicators. Without these interconnected elements, once products and services go wrong, all departments are passing the buck without an objective mechanism to find out the root cause of the problem, so they only take some stop-gap measures.

The problem is like a table tennis ball playing among the market, customer service, and the company. It comes and goes everywhere eternally and endlessly in a meeting or a report that makes (unnoticeable) improvements. Unsolved problems are like soulless ghosts floating around that unpredictably jump out to scare people every once in a while and destroy the corporate reputation and brand identity.

This phenomenon is widespread among companies, which exhausts employees in some departments and keeps business owners on tenterhooks all the time without knowing which and when the unexploded bombs are going to explode.

The Internal Customer is a Piece of Value Chain

Division of labor and process management are two basic rules of company management that cannot be removed, regardless of the scale or profession of the company. Specialty is the core foundation of functional organizational structure, and the process is how departments correspond through a project in the organization.

Functional organizational structure is generally divided into human resources, finance, marketing, research and development (or planning), production (or preparation), quality assurance, logistics, and service. These seemingly separate and independent departments have interconnected relationships that affect each other. Unfortunately, a clear connection between performance in various departments and the appropriate integration management are often unavailable in many companies' performance management.

When the marketing department gets the direction of future needs from market research, the R&D department must take action based on these needs other than a subjective idea they believe is the best. The two failures of Kodak and Nokia have clearly demonstrated the importance of directly catering market trends.

After the R&D department creates a product that meets customer needs, they have to produce the first batch of products to verify product suitability, system safety, and manufacturing feasibility first. Only when they pass these processes can they carry out mass production of the product.

The next thing to test after the launch of the product is logistics support, including packaging, transportation, replenishment of spare parts, support team deployment, maintenance and repair services, and market information feedback, which collaborates closely with product suitability and product quality level. Simply put, the results of the efforts made in the previous process determine how hard they should try to reach a desirable result in the following process. Furthermore, suitability and quality level both determine customer satisfaction with the company. However, if the direction of the market research is wrong, no matter how great the results of this whole process are, it still cannot grasp the real needs of consumers and the direction should be adjusted immediately accordingly.

This entire process is a closed loop in which each segment is tightly linked together. Without a connection between performance in the organization and the powerful system integration, it is impossible to bring all segments together and function well.

Running a business requires collaboration between many links. You fail if you get a wrong idea. —Konosuke Matsushita

Things Have Their Roots and Branches

There are two starting points for the production process, which may sound contradictory, but in fact, their goals are correlated. One is the goal of customer satisfaction, the other is the goal of products and services.

The goal of customer satisfaction is to meet the consumer's purpose of use, which meets the suitability of product or system and service that enables them to be used in complex usage environment to accomplish their tasks successfully. For example, the ability to conquer the challenge of producing a worldwide sold laptop that can be operated normally by different users in different industries under different climate and environmental conditions.

The goal of products and services is to meet the required specifications. Products should be manufactured in accordance with drawings and achieve functionality and quality requirements before the product leaves the factory.

The final result of these two starting points should be presented on the same product. How to do so? What is the priority order? As a matter of fact, these two things are two sides of the same coin: functionality and performance. Functionality refers to things that can be done; performance is the durability of those things, or in a broad sense: suitability (See *Chapter 7: Product and Service Suitability*).

When starting to plan a product or service, functionality is the first consideration—after all, without clear functionality, there is no way to make it a product or service—but the second consideration, performance (target goals), follows closely thereafter. No manufacturer focuses on functionality alone without considering performance. This is quite easy to understand: no customer is willing to buy a product that has powerful functions but fails within a short time, takes a long time for maintenance, and requires high maintenance costs.

In terms of consumption habits, product functionality can be ever-changing that allows customers to buy whatever features in a product they need and want. However, the performance requirements are never changed. No matter what features in products customers buy, they (both eastern and western consumers) all ask for the same performance requirement—durability. Cultural differences have no effect on this.

Many companies do not really produce their products as durable as that of international competitors for the following reasons: first of all, they see cheap as one of their competitiveness; second, one of their performance indicators is how fast their products can be launched and sold in the market. Together with the thinking that they can earn maintenance costs later or they want the product to be damaged faster so as to sell the latest version of the product. This short-sighted thinking is very different from consumer expectations, making it an impossible task for them to improve product performance.

Win-win Business Relationship

Companies in advanced countries have two functions: system integration and system assurance (i.e. the assurance of product performance-related capabilities, it is the collective term for suitability, safety, and support mentioned in previous chapters). Since there is the word *system* in both of them, these two functions cover the entire company's product management. System integration is the entire process of integrating and managing product development and production. System assurance is to ensure quality, safety, suitability, and other related performance.

Many companies in the manufacturing industry have simplified product performance and categorized it as a part of the quality department without fully carrying it out. The two management functions should plan, implement, monitor and improve, and adjust every project from the perspective of business operations. If these two functions are missing in brand management, then it is quite difficult for the company to become a stable and robust branded company.

Unfortunately, they are unavailable in most companies. When it comes to product R&D and manufacturing, what's in the project manager's head is still the three things mentioned in the *Introduction*: cost saving, instant profit, and low-quality standards without the concept of performance, not to mention the integration of functionality and performance. Furthermore, project managers usually work under the authority of a functional department in the manufacturing industry, so even they have the concept of system integration and system assurance, it is difficult for them to fully develop these ideas under the constraints of the functional department.

This is also the Achilles' heel for the Project Management Professional (PMP) system that is popular internationally. A lack of system integration and system assurance in the company is the reason why there are so many people who have the PMP certification want to implement project management but are powerless and unable to effectively promote it.

Internationally, system integration management and system assurance have already been developed and widely used in consumer electronics, various industrial products, machine tools and precision measuring tools, medical equipment, transportation systems, power and energy systems, chemical engineering systems, etc.

No One Cares as Long as They Have No Responsibility

I was sent abroad on official business for a year twenty years ago. I could not drive before, but whenever traveling with colleagues on a holiday or weekend, I always volunteered to drive when they were tired. One time, we had to drive on a curvy road near a cliff and it was quite terrifying. The colleague who drove were trembled with fear, so much so that he asked for someone else to take over and drive the car. The car was full of experienced drivers, but they were just looking at each other and no one wanted to drive. As I volunteered at that moment, I could not believe that no one objected the idea of me driving.

Another time was on a snowy day. We were driving on the highway and the road was covered with ice, so it was slippery. The same situation happened again. So I have got an observation: people would rather put their lives in others' hands and ignore the worst possible outcome just to avoid personal responsibility!

If everyone is passing the buck when they are in trouble, of course, they can expect there is someone enthusiastic and brave enough to take the responsibility for them or to let the senior executive take all the responsibility, but this is not a phenomenon a sound organization should have. It is also a taboo for system integration.

It should use the "goal of customer satisfaction" and "goal of products and services" mentioned previously in system integration to analyze, resolve, merge, assign duties, formulate specifications and objectives for specific functional subsystems, establish configuration management, conduct process and schedule planning, coordinate various interfaces, verify, improve, and finally, integrate evaluation and certification to see whether these two functions achieve the target goals set early. During the integration process, the company should conduct screening and matching for each department and even each employee in terms of responsibility, power, and capabilities.

With the advent of Industry 4.0 and 3D printing technology, the process of systematic management has been implemented in many manufacturing industries that are easy to achieve standardization. However, it still needs human power and human intelligence to complete the part that machines cannot do, such as the analysis and confirmation of target goals, validation of product and service specifications, interface coordination, configuration management, failure analysis, and improvement programs. It requires to pass the barrier of system integration before the traditional manufacturing industry can enter to Industry 4.0 and 3D printing, and it is impossible to get everything done by simply investing equipment!

Do not be Fooled by False Numbers!

There are numbers everywhere in the 21st century, but do not assume they all represent the truth. It is still quite difficult to make these numbers a reliable basis. If the data collection is incomplete or the data interpretation is wrong, the investment comes to nothing. If the customer 's needs are unclear, the brand identity falls; if the mass production lost basis, the production and sales are unbalanced. Low-quality standards reduces reputation; logistics supply emergencies drain your employees and lead to a reduced sense of unity; satisfaction indicators lead to falsehoods. These are problems caused by numbers.

It is the person in charge of the department who proposes the target numbers in goals and it is also the department that achieves these goals. If these numbers are either too difficult or too easy to achieve, then the person in charge should take full responsibility. If it is too difficult to achieve, it leads to fraud; if it is too easy to achieve, it wastes corporate resources, so that is way number is closely related to business administration. It all depends on system management and integration to rationalize numbers (goals and specifications), functions, professional energy, processes, and verification methods, as well as to make numbers generate meaningful connections.

Some of these numbers are related to the overall business strategy, product strategy, and even higher level and more long-term brand strategy. It is definitely not the boss or the project manager alone can handle and decide. Instead, at the management level, there has to be a permanent system integration organization that collects, organizes, analyzes data, and interacts with the company's executive level at all times.

Leadership Starts at the Top and Flows down

The most important thing to run a business is to set a vision and plan for development strategy. A vision is a long-term goal, and it is truly difficult to clearly develop future vision in the rapidly evolving and unpredictable market. But there has to be fundamental policy; otherwise, it is just like sailing without a compass—you can only go with the flow without knowing where to go.

A vision is how the company wants its image to be seen. Take Amazon as an example with its vision statement: "we seek to become Earth's most customer centric company, where customers can find and discover anything they might want to buy online." (from *Amazon.com*)

Under the guidance of the vision, all decisions can have a sense of direction and scope. This is very much like the constitution, the fundamental law, of the country and all laws derived from it must comply with the spirit and direction of the constitution. This is called the Rule of Law. It is the same for companies. There has to be an organizational vision and principles of behavior, which can be called as institutions, standards, and processes. But no matter how it is called; in short, it is organizational norms, and the important thing is it must be directional.

The importance of directionality is that changes in the market are complicated. There is always new information coming out, such as new technologies, new business models, new application market, new competitors and their new strategic direction, raw material sources and price fluctuations, new production techniques, new management theories, new laws and regulations, changes of the exchange rate, economic trends and so on. If the information is not well selected and organized first, it confuses people and makes them unable to decide which is correct. Until then, business decision-making is chaotic. At this time, the vision is brought into play and functions as a screening tool to rule out irrelevant market information, so it does not confuse the leader's mind.

If the senior executive cannot accurately take the direction or do not clearly understand the focus of the strategy, it drains and exhausts employees who implement them. What's worse is they may be forced to take responsibility for poor implementation, let alone there are some supervisors who do not do their job but stoop to flattery or get promoted through nepotism.

Looking at successful entrepreneurs of the older generation, were there so many "tricks" in management theory at that time? The way to success is to steady and practically head to the direction.

Regard Comments and Suggestions as Stepping Stones

There is a long and detailed process for the output of a product or system to go through:

1. Confirmation of requirements and operational objectives: list operational modes, environmental stress conditions, and possible risks.

2. Specifications: functional specifications, performance specifications, industrial safety and environmental protection specifications, material specifications, quality specifications, and test and acceptance conditions. These should be all clearly defined.

3. Management tools: system engineering management, project schedule management, interface management, risk management, configuration management, quality management, adaptive management, logistics management, operations management, maintenance and repair management, knowledge management, database management, etc. These management plans should be planned in advance for the project to be implemented smoothly.

4. Properly coordinate and balance conflicts between various operations if there are problems occur during the implementation process.

The four processes above are very intricately intertwined like a closely woven net. If any node on the net loosens, a big loophole can be found on it, making the product or system unable to produce the output or leaving unsolved troubles to customers. So if there is an error in any part—specifications, professional technique, process sequence, schedule planning, implementation resources, or human resources—that are not solved during the project process or not remedied later, problems that come with it are unpredictable.

What are the factors that prevent the real situation from being revealed? For starter, the attempt to run ahead of the schedule in the hope that the product can be quickly produced. In order to save time, it skips things that should be studied clearly for they are what customers expect to have, such as task types, operational requirements, and environmental stress investigation. This false first step guides all the following efforts in the wrong direction and produces a product that does not meet customers' needs. The second factor is the attempt to take advantage of others in the hope of minimizing the cost. So even with high-level requirements, they still try desperately to reduce the cost in every aspect, but usually, the case is that the lower the cost, the more difficult it is to reach the required specifications. No one wants to suffer a loss, so it eventually comes to a standstill that the supplier either is unable to successfully deliver products on time or ends up asking for extra money.

The next one is interface coordination, which sacrifices the part that is considered less important in interface conflict between functionality and performance. For example, when the operating speed requirements of the product are high, it is relatively easy for the temperature to be increased as well. However, it is not an easy task to dissipate heat because there are so many hot spots in the system with little space for heat dissipation device. So it tends to sacrifice the efficiency of heat dissipation (i.e. it does not matter if the temperature is slightly high), but the problem will occur more often on the sacrificed part in the future.

In such a complicated project, the opinion is the message received by the system, and the suggestion is the active analysis from a certain part of the system. Instead of seeing it as a challenge to the authority, the chief systems engineer should cherish the information and use it properly. If they possess all the expertise and resources needed, but lack ability to integrate or lack emotional intelligence, and, as a result, they cannot humble themselves to listen to the correct advice or they are reluctant to admit mistakes when making a wrong decision, but toughly forcing their team or the outsourcer to cooperate with them, then the whole team is snowed under with work by the time of delivery.

Resources and Supports

In a complicated or huge project, everyone's work is carefully divided with a clear responsibility, so everyone wants to do their job well. Working in an environment with limited resources, people fight over resources and there is even workplace bullying occurs when some colleagues are excluded.

What are these resources? For starter, power (or at least the right to speak). Power itself is an important tool that controls resources, so if one wants to control the lion's share of resources, the first thing to seize is power.

Everyone should contribute value to the organization, but those who like to seize power are mostly those who contribute relatively less value in the professional field. Fighting for power give them a sense of security for they usually think they have less favorable conditions for survival.

Conversely, some bosses also like to put their cronies or family members in key positions like personnel, finance or procurement. Since these people have special relationships with the boss, they are more reluctant to fully cooperate with the professional manager who is responsible for system integration, which makes it difficult to carry out the project successfully. Companies competing in the international market should keep up with international regulations and management models. For this reason, it is not a blessing if they have such members who cannot keep up with or even sabotage system integration.

The second type of resources is funds. Things that can only present their results in the long run are often unable to receive sufficient funds. For example, those been classified as performance such as suitability, logistics, and service. This mindset is exactly what damages the long-term endurance of products and services that affects their survival in the market, so what it truly damages is the brand identity.

The third type of resources is professionals. For those of the "cheap and cheerful" mindset, the easiest things to implement is working overtime and optimizing manpower utilization. In the Chinese culture, people regard the act of providing work opportunities as "the boss is offering the employee a free meal" rather than regard it as a fair deal that "the boss is paying money in exchange for service." The consequences of the average wage of the country being lower than that of the same-level countries are a growing gap between the rich and poor, brain drain, low consumption rate, and even a vicious job-hopping cycle. These are the bitter fruits all companies taste, not just unfavorable for a single company in the long run.

The difficulty of system integration lies in gaining and proper using resources. Since the above problems are not what can be easily overcome by project integrators with their levels in the company, it requires the top-level management to pay special attention to the resources allocated for system integration and fully support it.

Redefining CEO

Usually, when the company's board of directors decides to hire a new CEO, the company is almost helpless. By introducing an outsider to rectify the situation, they can avoid all personnel burdens and easily make up their mind resolutely. One of the most terrible aspects of capitalism is the practice of Chief Executive Officer (CEO) which I jokingly call it as the Chief Execution Officer who carries out a death sentence. It is because when there comes such a new person in a company, it always comes with layoffs, integration, demotion, and pay cut. The job you originally have may disappear overnight, and as it changes or disappears, the innocent family and children are also stuck in a miserable situation.

The annual salary of a CEO in an international company can be as high as several million or even tens of millions of dollars, which is used as a quid pro quo with the CEO for greater performance. This is why the new CEO tries to make achievements as soon as they take office. Based on this premise, employees cannot even put up little resistance to it, and the tangible and intangible harm is really indescribable.

Does this really benefit the company? It is a matter of debate. The affirmative side still insists on the highest moral goal of the company—maximum interests—mentioned previously in this book. Under this goal, the department with a deficit or no performance improvement for a long time is immediately laid off. For departments with too many redundant employees, they tend to set a random target number of employees and ask these departments to achieve it. On the other hand, the opposition side hopes to re-examine the business and management problem from various aspects to find out the root cause and give the right solution. They object to the idea of indiscriminately sentence them to death because this greatly causes problems for employees' future career prospects and their families.

There was a newly appointed CEO who went into a department at the time nearly the flexible working time and counted the number of the employees in the office. Then he took that number as the number of employees the department could have while the rest were otherwise all laid off. There was another CEO in another company who stipulated that if an employee who was offered a certain amount of salary or has attained certain seniority could not make sufficient profit of the current year at least as high as the salary they received, they would make this employee walk the plank, no matter how many other important human assets there were in this person.

Another case happened in a multinational company where the new CEO imposed a hiring freeze, so when one of the departments suddenly had more orders, it was not allowed to hire new employees but to reduce the workload of other departments and dispatch their workforce to help. The question is, did these employees from other departments have the expertise and experience needed for this department? For the new CEO, the answer was: it is none of my business!

It is unnecessarily for brand management to always take humanity concerns as a top priority; but instead of being a merciless judge who finds every employee who earns little profit guilty, it has to be at least operationally reasonable. For example, what is the outlook of the department with a deficit after conducting the review and analysis? What is the reason for the deficit? Is there any room and opportunity for transformation? What is the reason for no performance improvement for such a long time? Is it because the direction is wrong, the resources are insufficient, the product is not good enough or the leadership and management is poor?

Liabilities Flow Along With Assets

A product with a long lifecycle and requires continuous maintenance is mostly a tool product that customers use to create business or mission-critical benefits. This type of products has gone through customer acceptance, but if it is already outside the warranty period and one day the product is broken, what does the customer do? The first thing comes to their mind is to call the agent or the original manufacturer to repair it. If they cannot solve it, the level of dissatisfaction definitely rises.

This type of product is highly functional, costly, technically complex, rigorous in specifications; it relies on a complete logistics support system, requires to establish and store experience and data, and requires long-term spare parts supply. These products include weapons, machine tools, large vehicles (such as aircraft, ships, trains, and automobiles), factory equipment, large electromechanical equipment, facility, communication and signaling equipment, energy and power equipment, and even consumer electronics.

Manufacturers should determine the long-term support methods and performance objectives for these products in the marketing strategy to gain customer satisfaction and recognition. This involves the product's reliability, maintainability, safety, logistics support, maintenance services, spare parts supply, new technology enhancements, substitutability, scalability, and interoperability. The performance of these operations is also a competitiveness indicator for many international factories in the global market, otherwise they have long been expelled from the market.

If these elements are not considered clearly, they either dissatisfy the customer or cause chaos in the internal management of the company. Either way, it increases unexpected costs and greatly decreases profit margins of the company. They are connected with the long-term development and planning of the company, which start from brand policy, to marketing strategy, to product strategy, then to service strategy, and eventually they should be handed over to the system integration department to be implemented. This is why system integration must be closely coordinated with the operational and management levels mentioned in the previous sections. Without this series of policy and strategic thinking, decision-making, planning, and implementation, companies can only take stop-gap measures and never be able to develop international competitiveness. Now we can clearly see how heavy the responsibility of the system integration department is.

Likewise, users of these system products also have to establish a corresponding system integration department to continuously collect data for observing, analyzing, and reviewing the cost-benefit of these system products used for their own business operations. Once the cost-effectiveness is found to be insufficient, it requires to analyze the cause, collect evidence, and file a complaint with the supplier for improvement. As a supplier, if the company does not know how to set up system integration, it lose its competitiveness. On the other hand, as a buyer, if the company lacks the ability of system analysis, its investment is wasted and the supplier is constantly making endless demands on them.

The World is Gradually Eliminating the Need for Middlemen

Human societies have evolved from clan societies to the modern ones, in which the priority and distribution of power and resources are all determined by social status. Under backward production conditions, the traditional organizational structure is pyramid-shaped with a narrow top and a wide bottom—the top is the executive level, which gives orders, and the bottom is the operational level, which works hard. Both of them are clearly defined without any ambiguity. What's confusing is the middle level.

The middle level is responsible for management work. The policy is formulated by the executive level, and the middleman has to use the power they hold to fulfill policy tasks. They are responsible for the success or failure of policy implementation, and at the same time they have to manage the results produced by the operational level to meet expectations of the executive level. So here comes some interesting situations.

Challenges for the middle-level managers are: is it possible for them to fully understand and grasp the upper-level policies and intentions all the time? Do they have leadership skills? Do they have planning and management skills? Do they have professional guidance skills for implementation? When examining middle-level managers with these questions, they can roughly carry out 90% of capacity assessment in middle-level management. For the upper-level, these people are their subordinates; for the lower-level, they are their leaders. If looking from the perspective of human nature that pursues good fortune and avoids disaster, what do most people in this level do under such a situation? The position advantage they can most easily gain is to let the decision be made by the upper-level and let the result be produced by the lower-level. In this case, they can assign responsibility to the lower-level and take credit from the upper-level. Over time, it naturally forms a unique middleman culture in the organization, which often leaves no trace of damage to the organization, but the outcome is always fatal.

Just take a look at the example of Nokia's failure. Quy Huy, a professor of strategic management at INSEAD, concluded in the research of Nokia that the spread of fear among the company's middle management and senior executives is the reason for its failure in the battle of the smartphone. It caused laziness in the entire company, making them incapable of responding to Apple's game-changing devices.

After interviewing 76 senior executives, middle managers, engineers, and outside experts, he discovered that this "organizational fear" was deeply rooted in this type of culture: working with moody leaders and frightened middle managers makes them too afraid to tell the truth. In this way, a classic history was written and became a lesson plan for various corporate research institutions.

Situations are changing rapidly in the 21st century. There is no time to wait for middle managers to serve as a bridge between the upper and lower levels. In addition, the fact that the technology of Industry 4.0 and Internet of Things combines with standardization, modularization, and timely informatization of specifications and implements work under a highly automated environment declines functions and contributions of middle managers and makes them gradually fade away from history.

Chapter 11

Sustainability Management

How does a century-old business continue to survive?

According to the research published in *Harvard Business Review* in April 2013, things that make companies exceptional around the world are consistent with the following three basic rules:

1. Better before cheaper—in other words, compete on differentiators other than price.
2. Revenue before cost—that is, prioritize increasing revenue over reducing costs.
3. There are no other rules—so change anything you must to follow with Rules 1 and 2.

The abilities to grasp market demand all the time, meet customer's expectations, strictly follow the code of ethics, and fulfill social responsibility are the collective experience of branded companies in all countries at all times. The difference is that since communication and transportation technology are well developed nowadays, it is really like what they say, "distance cannot keep us apart" for commercial services. However, international regulations are getting more stringent as trading is getting way more prosperous than before, posing a more complex and difficult challenge for modern sustainability management.

Nevertheless, the three brand elements (i.e. quality, character, and taste) mentioned in *Chapter 1* still play a very important role in running a business. In order to enable the century-old brand to maintain its sustainability management, there are things for these elements to be actively done and avoided.

What modern companies lack is not scientific and technological knowledge, or policies and regulations; what they truly lack is the code of conduct of being proactive and the cultural quality of being pragmatic. These are in fact the most decisive conditions for a company's success, and without them, even a company with best policies and regulations still fails anyway.

In order to improve brand connotation and cultural quality, you need to first be sincere and open-minded to examine the "value corruption" phenomenon derived from the pursuit of business interests, then truthfully introspect and improve yourself. The common value corruption phenomena I have seen in many companies are generally:

1. Short-sightedness: the management level only cares about short-term performance and profit. They do not care about substantive content nor future development.
2. Disunity: all departments are independent of each other. They pay attention to the performance of their own business and do not care about the overall development of the company.
3. Buck passing: they tend to outsource important work (responsibility) and value external appearance over core company values.
4. Ignorance: they do not respect and follow international regulations, and they also ignore long-term accumulation of experience and employees' opinions and talents.

5. No principles: no moral sense and self-esteem, find loopholes in the law, hypocritical, mutual flattery, phoning it in.

It is necessary to improve these phenomena if the company wants to enhance the competitiveness of the brand and shack off the powerlessness.

Cogito, ergo sum

"If you know the enemy and know yourself, you need not fear the result of a hundred battles," said in the Art of War by Sun Tzu, which points out the first key to all types of competition: who am I? And the next question is: what do I want to do, and why? Then ask: who are the competitors and what are they doing? Last, considering your own abilities, energy, and resources to decide what role you want to play in the market and develop a strategy that makes you play that role.

This process can be applied to everyone and every company and organization because we all face problems of how to survive and how to live a better life. If you own a food stall, you maintain your own special flavor and join a well-known night market. If you own a Michelin-starred restaurant, you continue to improve your quality and taste. Do not randomly lower the prices and engage in sales promotion.

After knowing yourself, you need to know who your customers are. If you do not know the answer, it means you do not even know what customers need. It is also important to know where they are, so the channel is the key. All your efforts are in vain without channel (including e-commerce channels).

Besides customers, you need to know your competitors and compare their strategies with yours to see whether they are different from, partially overlapped or in conflict with your competitive strategy. What are the things that make you believe you will most certainly win? Emphasizing on low price is in no way a good thing because it degrades the entire consumer market and brings down your business. You can emphasis on quality, lifetime warranty, and even perfect pre-sales, sales, and after-sales services. The important thing is to develop a strategy that creates brand values rather than to develop the one that makes a quick profit.

If everyone adopts a low-price strategy, it only lowers the overall market sense and ends up with chaos. No one benefits when every seller is lowering their price. Just take a look at all international products, have you ever seen a brand use a low-price strategy to seize market share?

The last thing is to know which direction to go in the next step. Technology and competition are changing with each passing day and market maturity is getting higher and higher, so it is impossible to maintain the market position all the time. Give yourself a vision!

It is Best for Family to Just be Family

The first barrier of sustainability management for a family business is siblings working together or separation of powers. For family members who run a business together, the most important thing is not to fight one another. No matter what kind of container it is, as long as there is a crack in it, it leaks—it is only a matter of time.

There are many famous royal sibling rivalries in history, so does in modern family businesses. Sibling is just a general term, here it refers to all family members that can have a similar competitive situation in business either in the past or in modern time. There were inevitably many killings between relatives even with a strong binding force of family in medieval feudalism, not to mention that this force is almost disappeared when ethics and seniority in the family are less important in modern time.

The legacy of history and culture, however, is not completely disappeared. Instead of choosing a successor based on talent and ability, the continuation of most family businesses is still basically using seniority succession. If the successor is incompetent or the distribution of power, rights, and interests does not satisfy most people, then the talented people will try to carve out a niche for themselves or try to replace the successor or rest on their laurels in the company, which buries the root cause of misalignment or competition in the workplace.

This situation interferes with the development direction and management system of a company and weakens their devotion to brand policy. Although a large number of medium and large companies have given up the family-owned business model, there are many SME owners who cannot let go of their power still embrace the idea of patrimonialism and bite the bullet. The common practice in these companies is to let the next generation start as an entry-level employee in the company and promote them after a period of time. This is called successor development. But how many better professionals should they surpass during this training process, and what is its effect? Well, it is only a matter of opinion.

Is there any other relatively good way to solve this problem? The best one has actually long existed! The professional manager system adopted in many companies in Europe and the United States is generally choosing by talent and ability which allows the professional management team to take over the whole business without the family meddling in it (they are at most supervisors of the company). By doing so, the family members can both avoid disrupting professional business operation and receive the company's profits, thereby avoiding negative effects caused by family competition and sustain the company's brand.

Carry Through to the End

There was a famous quote said by a robber when he robbed the bank:

"Freeze! The money belongs to the state, only life belongs to you!"

~~ Words at the key moment should hit the nail on the head~~

The robber in this joke must be a leader. He could still control the whole situation with a simple and easy-to-understand sentence even when everyone at the scene was in a panic. This is leadership.

Charisma is a necessary trait for a business leader to achieve stable development, especially when the company is experiencing severe challenges, the leader can get straight to the point and make decisions calmly, rapidly, and correctly. When the Republic of China (Taiwan) withdrew from the United Nations, Chiang Kai-shek, the President of the Republic of China at that time, encouraged the whole nation and easily calmed people's hearts with simple words. Meanwhile, he sent people to the United States to learn about semiconductor manufacturing and planned the Ten Major Construction Projects in Taiwan which laid the foundation for Taiwan to create a world-known economic miracle.

In the summer of 1929, the United States was still living and working in peace, but on October 24, 1929, it created a widespread financial despair and suffocated the country's economy all of a sudden. That day was later known as "Black Thursday" in American history.

President Roosevelt immediately and urgently launched a series of measures, known as the New Deal, which not only saved the country but also established a solid national strength for World War II twelve years later. Otherwise, world history would not be the same. This showed how influential the power of a good leader can be.

It relies on wisdom, the ability to see the big picture, foresight, willpower, ambition, execution, and more importantly, the ability to serve as a role model for a good leader to be faithful to their word and set the tone for their team. Regardless of the scale of the company, these are things every boss or every person in charge should prepare:

- ❖ Create a vision and set a direction
- ❖ Serve as a role model and practice what you preach
- ❖ Good at motivating people and have a can-do attitude
- ❖ Not afraid of challenges and face it with perseverance
- ❖ Cultivate people's talents and consistently achieve high performance

No Pain, No Gain

For most companies, one of their weak spots is the human asset. According to MBALib, *human asset* refers to "labor resources that a company has or controls in a certain period of time which can be measured in monetary terms and bring future economic benefits. It is the capitalized form of the investment in human resource; in other words, the human asset is the total cost a company spends on recruitment, selection, hiring, training, and development. Human asset is a type of human resource;

it is a special asset of a company that has potential future benefits or potential profitability."

It can be said that after deducting fixed assets from total assets, most of the remaining assets of a company are considered as human assets, including institution, culture, patent, intellectual property, and experience database. Human asset is contributed by all staff and it can bring tangible and intangible benefits to the company as a whole. In addition to measurable economic benefits, there is also brand reputation and identity gained in the market.

Giving the corresponding remuneration for employees as much as the responsibility they should take is called *consideration*. The employment relationship is a type of transaction, so it should also follow the principle of fairness. Modern companies have already developed a complete personnel system, so the important thing for the owner to pay attention to is factors that undermine the effectiveness of the hiring system, such as:

- Exploit employees;
- Intentionally ignore or reduce the contribution value of employees;
- "First come, first serve," and choose by seniority;
- Employee inbreeding that produce a factional culture (factionalism) and cause internal troubles in the company;
- Office politics;
- Unequal power is no equality and it leads to the abuse of entrusted power for private gain;
- Apotheosis that kills creativity and suggestions;
- A top-down rewarding and bottom-up punishment system.

If the owner can prevent the occurrence of these phenomena as much as possible and allows employees to make full use of their creative potential and satisfy their self-actualization needs (the final level of Maslow's hierarchy of needs), then they can do their best at work.

Do to Others as You Would Have Them Do to You

Salaries and wages are one of the operating costs that is often placed in icy financial statements together with material costs, equipment costs, administrative costs and so on. When these other costs are to be reviewed or reorganized, salaries and wages are also placed on the same platform.

The hardware is cold while the human heart is warm and full of feelings; there is a big difference between these two. The cost of hardware or materials varies with market conditions, and various strategies can be used to reduce the costs when purchasing. But if the company applies this strategy to employees, the situation is changed.

There are specifications for hardware and materials that can be measured and estimated according to the market price, but people are different. They vary with personality, attitudes, family background, values, and loyalty. It can generate very different output values even with the same academic qualifications and seniority, thus, in order to maximize the benefits of human capital, they have to be treated with different attitudes.

Return on employee investment is very unpredictable. When they are not satisfied with the way they are treated, it is not easy to make them focus on their work, not to mention being proactive. They are unable to contribute wholeheartedly when they do not feel a sense of belonging in the workplace.

Speaking of a sense of belonging, it does not necessarily mean direct expenses like wages. It can also be the investment in the environment, compensation, benefits, learning, and development for employees; it can even be the investment in corporate culture, activities, and interactions. But the most important thing is to align employees' values with those of the company for it helps them to create a sense of belonging.

What are sources of a sense of belonging? First of all, the working atmosphere. In addition to a comfortable and safe work environment, it also includes respect for employees and the recognition of their positive performance. Since it is impossible to use specifications to regulate employees in the same way we regulate hardware, when a company hopes to increase productivity in employees, it does not realize that it has to give every employee time and space to learn and grow. Since employees are too scared and afraid to make mistakes in the environment where mistakes are forbidden to make, they develop the attitude of "the less you do, the fewer mistakes you make; the more you do, the more mistakes you make." This is the major invisible waste in organizations.

Secondly, salaries and wages. It is not just about making decent money to support the family, employees also want to see the reward they can get through hard work. Since 2012, many large US companies include Deloitte, Accenture, Microsoft, Adobe, Gap, and Medtronic have all announced their departure from the annual performance reviews that have been implemented for years and changed to new systems with more flexible and frequent communication and evaluation. One of the way to conduct employee performance appraisal is to provide instant feedback more often to recognize the contribution of employees so that they can feel they are treated fairly and boost a sense of belonging.

Some business owners believe that offering a job is like offering a free meal, they do not see employment relationship as an equal and fair relationship, so they tend to pay attention to customer value other than to employee value, making it impossible for them to share the wealth they earn together with their employees. They hardly realize that if employees do not feel the efforts they make are recognized, it is impossible for them to protect customer value for the company.

The last source is the spirit and culture of the company. Does the company have positive values? Do they respect humanity and society? Does the boss have a positive social image? Are the company's products and services beneficial to society?

If the boss exploits employees and takes advantages of them, employees will take advantages of customers, and customers will then take advantages of the boss. It turns out the boss loses in the end, so never treat employees badly or unfairly!

He Who Supports you Till the End is Your Biggest Asset

Character is the comprehensive quality of a person or an organization. Quality is the way a person treats other people, the environment, and their work with their own self-cultivation which is related to social ethics, laws, and values they have.

However, the influence of capitalism such as material consumption and the pursuit of money has made everyone leave self-cultivation behind. When people focus on chasing material enjoyment and wealth, they are not only unable to settle down but they also fail at work and in life. In this case, is this life worth living?

There are companies that boast about their achievement of creating jobs, prospering the economy, and contributing to society, but the question is—how they treat their employees? Have they considered the reasonable output of human assets? Have they considered the balance between spiritual and physical health? Have they considered the employees' relationship with their family members? Have they considered the stability of the whole society? Have they considered whether there is a brain drain in the company? If these answers are no, please give the private time and space back to employees. There is a lack of corporate character if the cost-saving measure of the company is so strong that it affects the quality of life of employees.

Honesty is the Best Policy

The consequences of dishonesty are extremely serious, so much so that it can erode fundamental principles of the country.

When everyone takes profit as top priority and sees hypocrisy as nothing big deal, the society falls into corruption and decay. It is like every company is illegally pouring wastewater into the river without filtrating it, so it pollutes the source of safe drinking water and harms the ecosystem. Isn't it the same for the country and society? Our society loses its vitality completely if it is full with hypocrisy. What makes matters worse is the next generation will find it harder to clean up the mess made by the previous generation because they are also accustomed to this phenomenon that they neither think it is a big deal nor think they can do anything about it. This is a major retrogression of civilization and the consequences are disastrous.

So does this situation have anything to do with the brand? Of course! It definitely reduces economic strength and overall consumption and leads to low investment, fewer tourists, reduced export orders, more security incidents, and more food safety incidents, making people want to leave their own country. Integrity sounds like some sort of homework of a primary school student that is not worth mentioning after the exam, but if adults do not act in good faith, the country is in a real crisis.

Integrity is the quality of being honest and having strong moral principles that should be the highest ethical standard in all fields.

Soft Power is the Nutrient of Hard Power

Whenever there is a branded company, there is a brand culture. Positive connotations of business cultures that are shared in all countries at all times can be categorized into the following five points:

1. Seeking truth from facts: whatever you do, be sincere and truthful, do not be hypocritical.
2. Putting quality before quantity: do not over promise; your actions should match your words;
3. Rather slow than hurried: be well-prepared for everything; the more haste, the less speed;
4. Reasonable and transparent: clarify internal powers and duties; do not use your advantage to oppress others;
5. Fairtrade and fair benefit: benefits and obligations should be equal and transparent.

Behind business operations, there must be values, concepts, styles, and principles that affect all aspects of the company's business direction, major decisions, systems, processes and so on. These are elements that establish a corporate culture. If it is a good culture that allows the company to accumulate brand equity, it is the soft power of the company. As the Chinese saying goes, "the superiors' virtue is the wind, and the inferiors' virtue is grass. Wherever the wind blows, the grass bends." If the company wants to receive good evaluation for its brand, it should first recognize the value of correct values and the power of corporate culture. Superiors need to start with themselves to motivate the entire company and rebuild a strong cultural atmosphere.

Success May Also be the Mother of Failure

"Resting on our laurels" is a common phenomenon, especially for those who have participated in the entrepreneurial stage. These people have experienced various difficulties and challenges in the pioneering stage, and when they succeed, it seems natural for them to take the valuable experience of success at that time as criterion and truth.

A company has to go through a comprehensive exploration to be established, including market demand, products and services, management models, financial scheduling, and work team establishment. These entrepreneurs and pioneers have to come up with solutions for every new problem they have, and once the solution is feasible, it becomes a fixed model. But the question is this *new problem* refers to all challenges at that time, and *solution* refers to the mode and content they used to deal with that emergency. Together, it means to "find and implement solutions to challenges of the time."

What is the relationship between solutions at that time and current business operations? Now that everything is settled down and these solutions are turned into institutional process, what problems does it cause when following these solutions? The phrase *at that time* means when something happened in the past, so is it possible for them to be adapted to current situations that change rapidly on a daily basis?

Latecomers should always think about these things: has the consumer group changed? Has the consumer behavior changed? Have the competitive conditions in the market changed? Has the number of competitors increased? Is it possible for the latest or future development results in technology and management to be applied to your products and management, and what are their investment opportunities? Have your employees changed their values? How long can various old strategies, products, services, organizations, and processes continue to adapt to the competition? Be cautious and fearful! As the world is getting smaller and smaller, the life cycle of success is getting shorter and shorter, conditions for success are no longer the same.

Principle of Balance

It is uneven if there is no balance. Whenever there is unevenness, there is a struggle against this unevenness. This is applicable to people, events, and things.

Let's start with things. In *Chapter 7* (*Product and Service Suitability*), we talked about various product suitability which is the ability endowed in products to adapt to various challenges in various environment. Without this ability, the product fails; with the product fails, the customer is unsatisfied. As a result, if you can find a balance between product suitability and environmental challenges, then the product can function normally.

As for events, let's take the process as an example. If resources or efforts needed for a process are insufficient, there is no way to meet the requirements of the next process. When this happens, this insufficiency is passed down all the way to the end and even gets bigger and bigger, driving the whole situation out of control. This is what happens when there is an imbalance between the process and resources or practices. For example, if logistics support is insufficient, the service cannot be correctly provided. For more examples, please refer to problems mentioned in *Chapter 8: Logistics Support*, *Chapter 9: Market Services*, and *Chapter 10: System Integration*.

Then, let's talk about people. In commercial activities, there are buyers and sellers; the latter can be further divided into employer and employee. From the perspective of buying and selling, the price the buyer pays is in exchange for the results of efforts the seller makes. There is no such thing as "he who has the gold makes the rules." On the other hand, what the seller must do is to make a profit with the results they create and the results should be solid rather than falsified. Only when the two parties can build a consensus based on equality and sincerity can it be called as a good deal.

From the perspective of employer and employee, the employer also spends money buying contributions from the hard-working employee, so this is also a buyer-seller relationship with no one being superior or inferior. Responsibility and contractual obligations are the only things exist in this relationship—it does not show any status superiority. However, in some family-owned companies or traditional businesses, they use this attitude of "he who has the gold makes the rules" to manage employees, which is a violation of the contract and even against the humanitarian spirit.

The last one is workplace feudalism which has a great impact on organizations. There comes problems when living with the mindset that only highly educated people have the opportunity to serve as supervisors. Many people with high academic qualifications may not have all the planning, communication, and leadership skills to be a supervisor. However, in an attempt to gain a more advantageous position, good technicians have to give up their professional skills and join the competition to fight for a higher position that ends up causing chaos in business administration.

Confusing the division between management position and technical position is simply due to the fact that the wrong result is led by the wrong concept! If the company can balance rights and responsibilities with abilities and duties and put the right person in the right position, it can get the highest human capital return on investment.

Summary of the Nine Core Competencies of Brand Performance

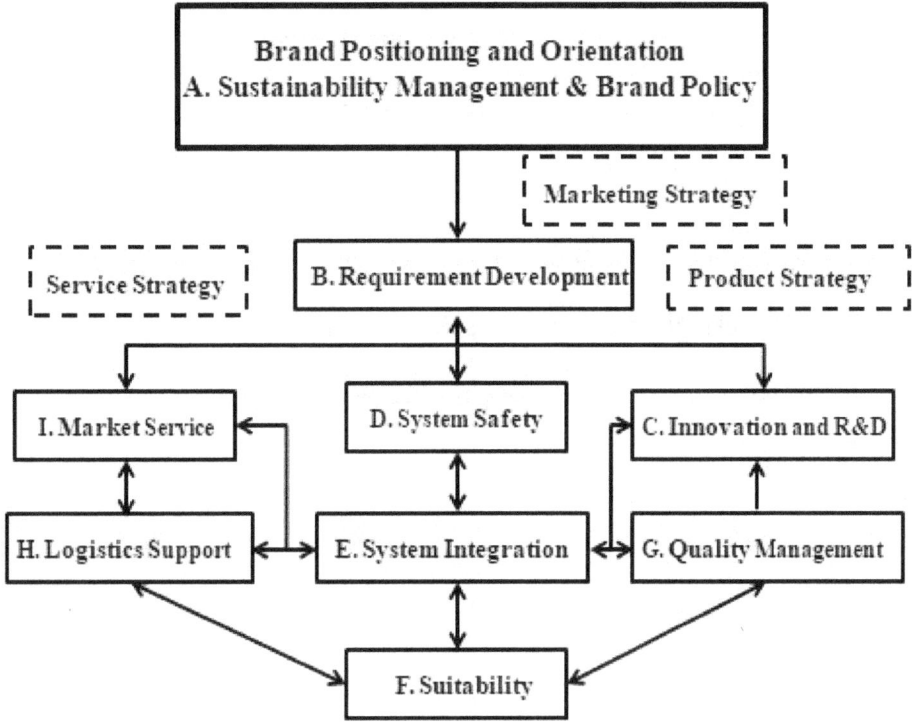

Flow chart of the core competencies of brand performance

The comprehensive description from brand attributes and positioning to the nine competencies is as follows:

1. Knowing who you are, who you want to be, and what brand you want to create.

2. Sustainability management: formulate a corporate vision, brand policy, and a marketing strategy; promote a corporate culture that values quality and character; create a brand management team.

3. Requirement development: establish a professional team to analyze needs; continuously focus on market needs, human needs, environmental requirements, and technical requirements to collect, sort, and analyze them; make an analysis report for the marketing strategy to be formulated and revised.

4. Innovation and R&D: establish a professional R&D team to conduct innovative research and development and develop a product strategy based on the needs and

requirements mentioned above.

5. System integration: establish a system integration team; develop a system integration framework structure, process, and management model; develop database management tools to integrate various requirements, designs, manufacturing, quality, product and service suitability, safety, and logistics in a project management system; develop product strategy.

6. System safety: establish a corporate safety committee to manage and supervise all safety-related matters throughout the company, including production, product, operation, maintenance, and business operations.

7. Product and service suitability: develop product and service suitability requirements for various needs and convert them into required specifications for product design. It plays a supervisory role in the system integration team to make sure the safety, suitability, and quality requirements are all met in the process.

8. Quality management: established a Quality and Failure Review Committee in which the general manager serves as the chairperson. Quality responsibility is directly delegated to all departments. Every head of the department is also the person responsible for the quality and the member of the committee. The quality department then functions as a professional consulting and verification department.

9. Logistics support: establish logistics support operations for the entire product life cycle (from R&D and manufacturing to the market); monitor the product and service suitability and material consumption and replenishment; provide feedback to system integration team; enter knowledge database to correct and update original integration results and revise related strategies.

10. Market service: develop a service strategy based on the results of various needs analysis, take them as a front-end reference for marketing strategy and product

strategy, and formulate and revise them based on the suitability performance and logistics support performance.

From these nine competencies, companies should develop key indicators based on their own characteristics and generate correlated indicators (i.e. arrows in the flow chart), so that the internal strategy process for the realization of brand policy can be fully and clearly monitored and controlled. For the management of indicators, you can consider these principles:

- Transparent performance management system
- Separate short-term and long-term performance records; the short-term ones should be instant rewarded but they only take a relatively small part of the overall performance
- Establish a visualization platform for the company-wide brand performance in accordance with the development of brand policy
- Traceable history records
- A report format that can be used in the decision support system

According to my observation and analysis to the engineering industry, the consumer industry, and the service industry, all business elements are logically the same but only vary with field, scope, and profession. Therefore, the application of business elements in brand performance theory is suitable for all industries or organizations.

"You can't manage what you don't measure," said Peter Drucker. When branding, you need to know what you are doing, how to do it, and then you have to measure it to know if you are doing it correctly. If you do not know how to do it correctly and your eyes are only fixed on market research data to "feel" how well you do it, then there is a lack of scientific view. It is pure luck when you success; it is a waste of investment and sabotages your brand when you fail.

The shortest distance between two points is not a straight line, but a tortuous one. When whaling in the ocean, besides a well-equipped boat and all necessary equipment, you also need satellites and sonar to correctly locate the whale. If you only want to eat a fish, you can do it with a fishing rod on the shore of a lake. But if you want to catch a whale with that, isn't it whimsical? The answer to how big the fish you can catch all depends on how well you prepare, not how well you can bluff.

Conclusion

BRAND—The Most Basic, Yet The Highest Business Strategy

Brand explicitly presents your entire content that cannot be hypocritical. The only way to a successful business is through improving the content and the strength of the brand rather than focusing on the appearance and external efforts.

After a brand is deeply rooted in the local market and firmly grasps the cultural complexities, it can expand into international markets. Even a service industry that does not have any product to produce carries its own cultural characteristics.

Instead of how to do it, you have to first ask why do you want to do it; otherwise, even with so many great tools available at your fingertips, you still do not clearly understand which one is the best for your business. Hence, do not be bewildered by the various business management tools. It is not that they are bad, but the most important thing is to uphold the spirit of seeking truth from facts to do everything pragmatically. By doing so, you can bring a bright future for your company. Otherwise, how is it possible for so many century-old companies established a hundred years ago when there were not so many theories at that time?

Every company can replicate tools and management systems, but not the values and philosophy of a brand. Only when the core values and core technologies are developed can a company truly creates its own competitiveness.

Companies should discover their unique self without relying on certification, evaluation, inspections or world rankings for self-affirmation. Paying attention to values, seeking truth from facts, striving for perfection, and building a brand step by step are, in fact, the real power and blessing for them!

www.ingramcontent.com/pod-product-compliance
Lightning Source LLC
Chambersburg PA
CBHW080909170526
45158CB00008B/2049